PELICAN BOOKS
A 346

HUMAN GROUPS

W. J. H. SPROTT

HUMAN GROUPS

W. J. H. SPROTT

PENGUIN BOOKS

Penguin Books Ltd, Harmondsworth, Middlesex
U.S.A.: Penguin Books Inc., 3300 Clipper Mill Road, Baltimore 11, Md
AUSTRALIA: Penguin Books Pty Ltd, 762 Whitehorse Road,
Mitcham, Victoria

—

First published 1958
Reprinted 1962, 1963

—

Copyright © W. J. H. Sprott, 1958

—

Made and printed in Great Britain
by Cox and Wyman Ltd,
London, Reading, and Fakenham
Set in Monotype Times

This book is sold subject to the condition
that it shall not, by way of trade, be lent,
re-sold, hired out, or otherwise disposed
of without the publisher's consent
in any form of binding or cover
other than that in which
it is published

CONTENTS

EDITORIAL FOREWORD

SOCIAL psychology today differs from the Social Psychology of the earlier decades of this century in two main respects. Firstly, its theoretical content is based on scientific evidence gained by planned observations either in field studies or through experiment. Secondly, it is more immediately concerned with the smaller and simpler face-to-face groups than with more complex organizations such as 'a nation' or 'society at large'.

Some of the classics of the old social psychology, such as Le Bon's *The Crowd*, McDougall's *The Group Mind*, and Ginsberg's *Psychology of Society*, may still be read with profit; but they do not tell us much that we did not know before or which we could not have known before if we had thought about the subject as much as had the authors of these works. These works were guides to systematic reflection. Their abiding value lies in their contribution to the analysis of some of the basic concepts required for the description and the ordering of the facts.

This volume is full of interesting factual material, but it also carries over to the new social psychology and applies to the study of small groups, this tradition of conceptual analysis. Indeed, the book opens with the discussion of one concept which is central to any kind of social psychology – the concept of a 'social group' and its distinction from a 'logical class' – a distinction simple enough to see and to state, but not so easy to apply in particular cases.

It was the Cambridge philosopher McTaggart who liked to illustrate the concept of a logical class by reference to 'red-haired archdeacons'. The class of red-haired archdeacons is just the plurality of individuals who both are red-haired and exercise archdiaconal functions. They do not form a social group, face-to-face or otherwise. They do not interact with each other in any context more than they interact with bald headed archdeacons or red-haired archbishops. So, too, with 'the Smiths'. The Smiths constitute a logical class the members of which have little or no fellow feeling for each other and do not interact with each other more than they interact with the Browns. But we must be careful. This is more doubtfully the case with the Campbells, the McDonalds, and the McGregors. And what about 'the pedestrians'?

Are they a mere logical class or a social group? If they are not a class conscious social group they may at any moment become one if motorists provoke them beyond the limits of their endurance. And if anyone thinks the question is of 'merely academic interest' he should take the cases of 'the People', 'the Workers', 'the Proletariat', 'the Bourgeoisie', and 'the Capitalists'. It is a bone of contention whether the capitalists are as innocent a plurality as the red-haired archdeacons or a genuine social entity interacting and cooperating in overt or clandestine ways to achieve some common purpose. So, too, are 'the workers' a self-conscious integrated group cooperating in the pursuit of worker-goals, or are they a simple logical class wishfully thought of by reformers as a genuine social group, or are they perhaps a logical class in process or becoming a real social group?

Such questions are illuminated in this volume by the new approach through the empirical study of small human groups. Its author has made observations of his own in the field, some of which are here recorded, which illustrate not only how social psychology has changed but also how the ideologies and the techniques of reformers and revolutionaries have been changed by the understanding of the psychology of small groups. Early revolutionaries and reformers thought in terms of 'humanity', 'the workers', and 'the people'. The new reformers are more concerned with the power that resides in the small communities of side streets and alleys. These powers can be observed producing their effects in Bethnal Green, in any American university campus, and in the 'Wards' of the Peoples' Republic of China.

22 May 1958   C. A. MACE

CHAPTER 1

DEFINING THE FIELD

This book is about human groups, and in particular about what sociologists call 'Primary' groups, that is to say, groups which consist of people in face-to-face relationship.

A group, in the social psychological sense, is a plurality of persons who interact with one another in a given context more than they interact with anyone else. The basic notion is relatively exclusive interaction in a certain context. You would say that the people working in a factory form a group because, in the context of their occupation, they interact with one another more than they interact with other people, so far as their occupation goes. Within the factory, men or women co-operating in a special job form a group – a sub-group with respect to the factory as a whole – for the same reason. A village may be said to form a group in this sense because there is more interaction between its inhabitants than there is between them and people living in the next village. A nation may be called a group because the members of the nation interact with one another more than they interact with the members of the nation across the frontier.

We have to put in the phrase 'in a given context' because, with respect to the smaller groups with which we shall be most concerned, a man may be a member of several groups. He operates as a member of his factory group when at work, as a member of his family group when he is at home, and as a member of his football team when he is playing football, or attending a meeting of the team.

This way of grouping people is, of course, not the only possible way, nor is it the only way which is of use to the sociologist and social psychologist. People can be grouped according to height or hair-colour, or any other physical characteristic, but such purely logical groupings are of little value because they tell us nothing more about the members of such categories. On the other hand people may be grouped according to occupation, sex, age, or social class, and such groupings may be important for various purposes; the sociologist may want to know about the number of women in employment, the relative numbers of the sexes, or the age-group structure of any society, while to say that a person belongs to a certain social class will tell us something about his way of life, his prestige, and his chances in life. In a large-scale society such as a modern nation, these groupings are not psychological groups in our sense. The miners of England do not interact with one another more than they interact with non-miners; the miners of the Durham coalfield do not interact with the miners of South Wales at all. Of course, the miners of a given pit form a group, but one which marks them off from those who work in a neighbouring pit. Adolescents do not form a group in our psychological sense, but in a village or in an urban environment there may well be psychological groups of adolescents. The members of the lower middle class do not form a psychological group, but if their interests are threatened in any locality they may form groups to protect themselves. Similarly women do not form a psychological group in the country at large, but women of like interest may form a Women's Institute in a rural area.

The criterion of relatively exclusive interaction in a given context has been chosen as the principal feature of psychological groups because it is quite clear that interaction is basic to the existence of groups; without some kind of interaction there could be no groups in our sense at all. Furthermore, when one looks about one, it is clear that interaction is not, as it were, evenly spread. If we could take a bird's-eye view of the globe from a great height we should see people, assuming we could distinguish them, moving about in relation to each other within confined areas with just a few moving across the edges into the next-door compartment. If we then came down closer to one of these areas, we should see them, again, moving about in relatively confined areas. Closer still we should see further coagulations, meeting and dispersing and joining up again into new formations. From a purely objective point of view such exclusive interacting pluralities would be obvious enough.

This objective criterion of interaction, however, is not the only one which social psychologists have picked upon as marking out one group from another. M. Smith[1], for example, defines a social group as 'A unit consisting of a plural number of organisms (agents) who have collective perception of their unity and who have the power to act, or are acting, in a unitary manner towards the environment'. In this definition the consciousness of the group as a group is the keynote. The members of a group, in our sense, are aware of their membership. This is certainly of great significance, as we shall see, but interaction must occur before the concept expressed by the word 'we' can be generated.

Again, in somewhat formal and distressing language, Morton Deutsch[2] defines a group as existing 'to the extent that the individuals comprising it are pursuing promotively interdependent goals', while according to the Freudian conception of the group 'two or more people constitute a psychological group if they have set up the same model-object (the leader) or ideals in their superego, or both, and consequently have identified with one another.'[3]

While not subscribing to Freud's account of the nature of groups, as expounded in his *Group Psychology*, we must accept his view that in all groups there is a moral element, there are standards or 'norms' of conduct incumbent upon its members to obey. We must, too, accept Deutsch's insistence on the fact that groups, in our sense, have purposes which are collectively pursued. Such purposes may be the furtherance of some interest, the solution of a task, even quite a small one, or the purpose of sheer survival. What these standards will be will vary from group to group, partly in terms of their past histories and vicissitudes, partly in terms of the particular task to be done, partly in terms of the dangers, if any, that threaten them from within or from without.

Thus we must think of groups as dynamic entities, and not as mere collections of people, haphazardly thrown together. Of course the urgency of their collective purposiveness will vary from situation to situation. The purposive unity of a village or a town may lie dormant for a considerable time, and it may affect individual villagers and citizens to different degrees, but it may be aroused in time of danger or when something that affects the unit as a whole presents itself. The threat of destruction from the air may lead to collective action, or to collective inaction if it is

11

thought that nothing of a useful nature can be accomplished. The hopes of a drainage scheme or the death of the Rector may lead to collective action or shared distress. But whether the members of a group are overtly engaged in the pursuit of a goal or not, their interactions are in part controlled by the standards of conduct current in the group.

The presence of standards of conduct is an essential feature of group interaction because interaction itself cannot go on for long without mutually accepted standards emerging. Standards have two aspects; they are frameworks of expectation and measures of esteem. If two people interact with one another, each has to adapt his response to the other, and so to behave that he can foresee what the other will do in response to his response. Theoretically speaking, each of the interacting parties has an enormous repertoire of behaviour, any one item of which he can call on at will, but it is obvious that if the behaviour of each were entirely random, they could never be said to *inter*-act. So it comes about that A will behave in a certain way calculated to elicit a certain range of responses from B, and B will, if he wishes the interaction to continue, respond to fit in with A's expectation more or less and to prompt A to respond in an appropriate fashion . . . and so on.

Of course, if you consider two people who belong to any culture – a system of standards accepted by the wide community of which they are members – meeting for the first time, it is perfectly true that they will be equipped already with expectations about each other. They will have learnt to deal with strangers, according to the rules of their larger group; that among other things is what 'manners' are for. Their initial contact, if they have been adequately trained, will be smooth enough; they will not have to develop standards of their own for the purposes of superficial or temporary interchange. If, however, they go on meeting, and form a group of two, each will have to respect the 'little ways' of the other; they will have common interests, in the arts, in sport, in financial enterprises or in anything else. Gradually mutual customs peculiar to themselves will be accepted by each, and form a set of mutually harboured expectations which form the standards of their interacting, over and above what one would call the 'common rules of politeness'. In addition, action in accordance with these standards will be regarded as 'right', and unexpected action, where an expectation is present, is something which has to be explained – it is somehow inappropriate and threatens the harmonious existence of the group. The significance of a framework of expectations can be seen when we reflect on the sentence: 'I can't get on with him, you never know how to take him', or 'you never know what he will do next'.

If standards of conduct, forming a framework of expectations, are required for the persistence of a 'friendship', it is clear that larger groups cannot do without them. There the situation is far more complicated. In a group of four, A has expectations about B, C, and D, and each of these has expectations about A, and each has to shape his conduct so as to fit in with the expectations of the others, and to elicit responses which will fit in with the expectations of all. The point is that they cannot keep together if each person behaves at random with respect to the others.

All this sounds very complicated, and of course complex mechanisms are at work, but in experience it is not complicated at all. What happens is that, without the participants noticing it, a set of customs becomes established which are regarded as 'right' within the context in which the group operates, and they are felt by each member as being in some sense outside himself. He does not think: 'I must do so and so because of B's expectation, C's expectation, and D's expectation'; he thinks, if he thinks about the matter at all: 'I must do so and so because it is *our* way of behaving'; or, 'because, if I do not, I shall let the group down', or 'because, if I do not, I shall get black looks'. The group, if it has been in being for a time, assumes a kind of independent existence in the minds of its members, and the rules are ascribed to it.

This is a somewhat sketchy account of the origination of norms of conduct in groups, as emerging from the prerequisites of persistent interaction, and more will be said about the matter later. It is also true that groups vary in the 'tightness' of their standards; some are more 'free and easy' than others, and some members may be tolerated by a group even though they behave, from the point of view of the group, very 'oddly'. All that is necessary at this stage is to realize that every group has some standards characteristic of it, and that it could not continue to exist unless this were so.

This point about groups having to have standards, and spontaneously generating them in the course of the interacting which is the basis of their existing at all, is important from another point of view. Because members of groups conceive of the standards of their groups as outside of them individually, because they can be put into words and communicated to a stranger or to a new member, and because they can be a matter of reflection and discussion, one easily gets the idea that they really do come somehow or other from outside. The individual may have intentions of his own which conflict with the standards of his group and he feels 'coerced'. The standards may, indeed, arouse such reverence that their origin is attributed to some supernatural being. This, of course, does not happen in the case of the smaller groups with which we shall be mainly concerned, but it does happen in the larger inclusive groups of which we are all members. When group standards are thought of as something apart from the interacting of the group members, we tend to think of them as somehow 'imposed' upon them. This gives rise to the notion that man is naturally unsocial, and that law-givers or moralists must come along and rescue him from his nasty brutish ways. This is nonsense. The generation of, and acceptance of, standards which regulate conduct and preclude randomness is, as we have already said, a prerequisite of social intercourse. The having of standards springs out of social intercourse; it is not imposed from outside upon it.

To say that all systems of morality spring out of social intercourse may, indeed, be going too far, but not so much 'too far' as might at first appear. Systems of morality involve two things: the obligation to control one's conduct in some way or other, both positively and negatively, and the obligation to do this particular kind of thing, and refrain from doing other particular kinds of things. The first element, the having of rules at all, springs from the necessities of persistent social intercourse. The second element, what the rules shall be, springs partly from social intercourse, and partly from reflection. Certain rules, such as the obligation to keep hostility by any members of a group down to a minimum, are required for the very existence of groups. Other rules which go beyond the mere survival of groups, and which may even prejudice their interests, derive from reflection. But the moral teacher, it must be remembered, does not teach in a vacuum. He can assume the idea of obligation as already there in the minds of his audience; what he sets out to do is to modify the content of the standards that have emerged out of the very nature of persistent living together.

This matter has been dealt with at some length because we shall come later to deal with experimental work on the pressure of group standards, and it is well to recognize at the outset that the having of standards and the sense of some kind of obligation to act up to them is part of the very nature of social, as distinct from 'feral', man.

We must now return to our groups. They are marked out in terms of differential social intercourse; their members have a consciousness of membership, which may, indeed, persist even when intercourse with co-members has ceased, as with an Englishman living abroad; they are purposive, though their purposes differ from one group to another, and they have standards of conduct in some ways common to many, in some ways peculiar to each.

In our examples of groups we have ignored the dimension of size; we have merely considered interaction. Now size is of great importance to us because by means of it we shall exclude a whole domain of groups from our consideration.

In the various attempts to classify groups, a distinction is made between 'primary' and 'secondary' groups, and between groups whose members are directly related, and groups whose members are indirectly related. There is an obvious difference between a nation and a Women's Institute or a school, or a discussion group. There is also a difference between a metropolis and a village. It is this difference to which the words 'secondary' or 'indirectly related', and 'primary' or 'directly related' refer.

The term 'primary group' was first used by Charles S. Cooley in 1909, when he wrote:

By primary groups I mean those characterized by intimate face-to-face association and co-operation. They are primary in several senses, but chiefly in that they are fundamental in forming the social nature and ideals of the individual. The result of intimate association ... is a certain fusion of individualities in a common whole, so that one's very self, for many purposes at least, is the common life and purpose of the group. Perhaps the simplest way of describing this wholeness is by saying that it is a 'we'; it involves the sort of sympathy and mutual identification for which 'we' is the natural expression.[4]

A primary group, therefore, is relatively small, and members of it can all have face-to-face contact with other members. This cannot be said of a nation or of a city or of a Trade Union or of a Professional Association. The unity of these 'secondary' or 'indirectly related' groups is mediated by symbolic means: a nation is a nation because its natives believe it to be a nation. A city is an agglomeration of houses with a fairly obvious visible boundary, but its unity as a secondary group lies in the fact that the citizens believe that they belong to Manchester, Birmingham, or London, while a conurbation, though also a built-up area with visible boundaries, is not a group in our sense because the people who live within it do not believe themselves to belong to it; they believe themselves to live in Walsall, Dudley, or Salford. Of course, the members of a face-to-face group, as we have seen, are conscious of its existence, and believe themselves to belong to it, but in addition to that, they are aware of the presence of the other members, which makes a great deal of difference. The 'secondary' group is, in a sense, purely a figment of the imagination. The reality is to be found in face-to-face interaction and long-distance communication.

Unity is further given to the secondary groups by language, by what we might call the 'chain-reaction' of social interaction throughout the group, and by unity of administration.

While it is true that a common language is not necessary for the existence of a nation-group – Switzerland bears witness to that – there must be some poly-linguistic communication possible for the idea of nationhood to become implanted in the minds of the nationals.

By the 'chain-reaction' is meant the social interaction which spreads throughout the nation by the agency of transport. It would be perfectly possible for a self-supporting community to remain completely cut off from the rest of the nation, in which case, strictly speaking, they would not belong to the nation-group in our sense; they would only be called 'Americans' or 'Englishmen' because they resided within a certain area of administration. So well-mapped are most countries that the existence of such remote and cut-off communities is highly improbable, but the notion is worth considering. The welding of all the persons within a certain geographical area into a nation-group is a function of communication. In the Middle Ages, when administrations were establishing themselves over areas similar to the political units of today, it is obvious that the idea of belonging to this nation or that was very unevenly spread, and may well have been restricted to the nobility and to such mobile merchants as there were. The peasantry in remote districts can scarcely have had much of an idea of belonging to this or that nation to which they owed allegiance.

Unity of administration, therefore, is not enough to generate the ideas and attitudes which are necessary for the existence of a nation as a secondary group. The old Austrian Empire could hardly be called one. Nevertheless unity of administration is important because it promotes interaction within its area and thereby paves the way for the idea of belonging to a nation to be engendered. Among the methods which are employed are a unified system of education in which the desired national unity is constantly stressed, the provision of common symbols, and the encouragement of attitudes of respect towards them. The central government of the U.S.S.R. is at the present time faced with this task, the task of welding the vast area from Minsk to Vladivostok, from Armenia to the White Sea into a unit. At first they displaced those persons in the various 'nationalities' incorporated in the Union who were, in their view, exploiting the people and who, therefore, would resist that full emotional incorporation which the administration wanted to establish. In the South they had to deal with feudal economies, and with groups bound by the bonds of kinship. They then tried to enforce a common language, but found this impossible. They have, however, established a uniform system of education, and a unified system of law watched over by the Procurator-General in Moscow, who reviews cases from

Tiflis, Irkutsk and everywhere else to ensure that a uniform set of rules is being administered. They have erected statues of Lenin and Stalin in practically every village throughout the Union. They arrange for peasants and workmen who have earned the privilege by hard labour to visit Moscow, where the great agricultural exhibition, with its pavilions of each 'nationality', displays the vastness of the empire to which they may be proud to belong. Besides this, doctors, technicians, and teachers, trained at the Centre, frequently spend part of their post-training career in remote regions of Siberia. By such means, assisted by a centrally controlled wireless and television network, and by increased communication by rail and air, they aim at destroying any chauvinistic attitude in the 'nationalities' and instilling a sense of membership of the Union, and a pride in such membership, in the minds of all the inhabitants of that enormous area. It will be seen that one of the most important methods is the promotion of what we have called a 'chain-reaction' of intercourse throughout the whole population.

Social scientists attempt to deal with these secondary groups by constructing schematic models of social structure and their interrelated social institutions by means of which the actual observable happenings can be explained. They note that certain problems face every society or group of this kind: the regulation of sexual intercourse, the provision of children and their social training, the exploitation and distribution of their resources, the organization of social interaction so that it may proceed smoothly towards whatever ends are in view, and a system whereby quarrels are settled and deviations from the rules are dealt with.

Every such group has socially accepted methods of dealing with these problems – its institutions, and the aim of the sociologist is to construct a coherent scheme which will display the interrelatedness of any set of institutions, to show which forms are incompatible with which, and what is likely to happen when the form of any one institution changes. And not only what happens to other institutions, but also what happens to the structure of prestige which we call the 'class structure'.

All this is the task of the sociologist, and it will be noted that he is not primarily interested in social interaction as such, in the way in which people affect one another when they meet together. Certain psychological assumptions, to be sure, may enter into the sociologist's considerations. Every society must cater for certain rather vaguely enumerated human needs. It is assumed that on the whole, if there is differential distribution of rewards, resources, and power, those who have most will seek to hang on to it, and those who have least may complain unless they are kept quiet. Such are about all the psychological concepts which the sociologist uses. The details of social intercourse are the province of the social psychologist. This does not mean, of course, that no reference to social psychological matters will be found in sociological text-books; they are there because the two disciplines overlap, but they are not the main business of the sociologist.

Similarly, in dealing with the other secondary group we have mentioned, the city, the sociologist is interested in finding out whether there are general rules of development. There are business areas, slum areas, 'residential' areas, suburban areas; do these change in relation to one another in an orderly way as the city expands? He is also interested in finding out whether there is a differential distribution of crime and disease, and he may be interested in the practical problem of reconstructing cities so as to ease the flow of life within them. Again he is not primarily interested in social intercourse, but rather in the framework within which social intercourse takes place.

Now this last sentence may prompt hot denials. What, it will be asked, about the work of sociologists on housing estates, to which, indeed, we shall be referring later on? Such investigations are certainly concerned with interaction, with neighbourliness, and with mutual dislikes. The answer is that in so far as they are concerned with the details of interaction, they are 'doing' social psychology, no matter what they call themselves. The smaller the area investigated, the more actual interaction must come into the picture and the closer, therefore, the investigation comes to being social psychology. It is, of course, waste of time to quarrel about names, but one point is quite clear: the study of social interaction is one thing, the study of the framework of institutions and urban areas in which it takes place is another. We shall be concerned with the former and not with the latter.

In making this distinction it must not be thought that we have given a full account of the problems which usually come under the heading of 'sociology'. No mention has been made of demography, the study of population, or of criminology, or of such enquiries as are made into the working of the welfare services, the structure and function of trade unions, or the degree of social mobility from one age to another. All that was required was to distinguish between the study of secondary groups and the study of primary ones.

We now, however, have to face a tiresome difficulty. In the whole range of groups, where do 'secondary' groups end and 'primary' groups begin? Groups which are small enough to meet in a room, where their interaction can be observed, are obviously 'primary'; they are, indeed, literally 'face-to-face'. A small village, a street, a 'neighbourhood', a school, a university, a small town come into the mind. But how small must the village, the 'neighbourhood' and the town be? The answer is vague: it must be small enough for almost everyone to know almost everyone by sight, and this may well be influenced by the amount of coming and going that occurs, by the degree of isolation, and by such chance circumstances as may have drawn an unexpectedly large number of people into interaction with one another. We have, in fact, to admit that we are dealing with a continuum stretching from clear cases of secondary groups at one end to clear cases of small primary groups at the other, with a vague area somewhere between them.

Before we leave the secondary groups we must notice the relation between them and the primary ones. During the course of ages every nation-group has developed a system of standards. Sometimes they are, or have been, homogeneous, in the sense that almost everyone accepted the same set, or at any rate paid lip service to it. Nowadays, except, perhaps, in Communist countries, the current standards are mixed, some people accepting one set, others accepting another. This plurality of standards is frequently deplored, by those who stress differences rather than similarities. In fact there is a good deal of common ground which is so ingrained as to pass unnoticed. There is in England, for instance, agreement about obligations towards children, about that respect for individual claims which we call 'fairness' or 'justice', about solving quarrels by negotiation or arbitration rather than by force, and so on. There may be disagreements about sexual standards, about how hard one ought to work, and about areas of condoned dishonesty. But whatever the complex mixture of standards, some common to all, some peculiar to different categories, the members of our primary groups are all of them brought up to have certain standards, or a selection of standards, which are current throughout the whole nation-group to which they belong. The standards of the primary groups do not develop in a vacuum; they develop within the general system of standards of the secondary groups in which they are incorporated.

This means that what can be discovered about small groups in one culture may not be applicable to small groups in another. Cross-cultural comparison alone can settle that. It also means that when considering the influence of a group upon its members, we must be careful not to think of them as blank sheets of paper; they are Americans or Englishmen as the case may be, and as such they arrive already equipped with such standards as they have derived, through their parents, teachers, schoolmates, and friends, from the common stock. This does not mean that primary groups play no part in what one might call the 'general socializing' process; on the contrary, they play a vital part. It is, in fact, in the primary group that the general standards are learnt, practised, and reinforced, but in addition pressure is brought to conform to the special standards which characterize the particular group in which a person may be. It is hoped that by holding the general standards constant, and studying the pressure to conform to the special standards, some light may be thrown on the inculcation of the former. The general standards, however, are not only learnt through precept, reward, and punishment administered by other people; they are also learnt through literature as well, and in every individual the form they take may well be modified by reflection.

Finally, there are one or two formal remarks which should be made about primary groups. They differ from one another in at least two dimensions. We may distinguish between 'natural' and 'artificial' groups; the former, like a village, or a street in a city, just grow by people coming to live there, or being born there and continuing to live there. Of course, villages may be deliberately planted, and housing estates deliberately populated, but after a time the inhabitants just live side by side because they do. This is clearly quite different from an 'artificial' group in a psychological laboratory, or a boys' camp, or any other group which has been deliberately formed for a special purpose.

Again, there is a temporal dimension. A village, a school, or a club may persist with varied membership, while a committee or a discussion group often exists only when the members are sitting round a table.

This means that the sort of problem relevant to each situation will differ, and the principles which can be investigated will differ. A discussion group presents problems of discussion, a housing estate presents problems of neighbourliness, while a gang or a camp may present problems of leadership.

In the following chapters an attempt will be made to describe the findings of social psychologists in several of these fields of group activity.

CHAPTER 2

THE MEMBERS OF THE GROUP

WHEN we think of a normal human being we think of a person who can walk and talk, reflect and reason, and who is aware of himself as a person, thus rendering him capable of pride and shame, ambition and disappointment. Human beings vary in their capacities for reasoning, in the ideas they have about themselves, and in their proneness to worry about the figure they are cutting, but some capacity to do these things at all is demanded of them if they are to be regarded as normal specimens of their kind. So much do we take these capacities for granted that we tend to think of them as somehow naturally emerging as the infant grows up.

The purpose of this chapter is to show that the characteristics which make the featherless bipeds, which we 'naturally' are, into 'human beings' are derived from social intercourse.

The infant has no idea of himself as a separate individual, it is a bundle of needs arising out of inner tensions, and capacities to respond to stimulation. It is not an 'I'. Psychologists who have made a close study of children are agreed upon this. A distinct awareness of oneself as a separate entity, says Piaget,[1] is the 'result of a gradual and progressive dissociation and not a primitive intuition'. Gesell, again, tells us that during the first year of life the child 'makes very meagre distinction between himself and others. His vocalizations are only beginning to have a social reference'.[2] At eighteen months 'His social insights are not much more brilliant than his perception of elimination functions. He is self-engrossed (not selfish) because he does not perceive other persons as individuals like himself'.[3] At two years 'Pronouns, "mine", "me", "you", and "I" are coming into use approximately in the order just given. . . . He is much more prone to call himself by his given name: "Peter slides down", instead of "I slide down".'[4] Such quotations can be multiplied from the literature on child psychology. They pose us, however, with a question: how does this sense of 'I' and the distinction between 'I' and 'me', the power, that is to say, to take oneself for an object, come about?

Part of the dissociation of the child from its environment doubtless comes about through the distinctive properties of the sense of touch; when we touch ourselves we feel ourselves being touched and we feel the touch of ourselves, when we touch something outside us there is only a single reference. This, however, is clearly not enough. For a full sense of 'I' social interaction is required. It is not easy to see how this comes about, but an illuminating attempt to account for it was given by George H. Mead,[5] in a book called *Mind, Self, and Society*. This is a somewhat difficult book, and only a brief account of Mead's general argument can be given here. In the first place he points out that non-human animals interact with one another in the sense that the behaviour of one acts as a cue to the behaviour of the other. This happens when cats play, dogs fight, or any pair of animals engage in sexual intercourse. We imagine, rightly or wrongly, that they act without *intention*, that they do not deliberately call forth responses in the way that human beings indubitably do. What, then, is peculiar about human interaction? The peculiarity, according to Mead, lies in the meaningfulness of the gesture, especially the 'gesture' of speech. The human being, he says, makes gestures which are *calculated* to elicit a response. This comes about by his 'taking on the role of the other' with whom he is interacting. He has already had experience of responses called forth by his spontaneous behaviour, but gradually he acquires the capacity to respond himself in a kind of imaginative way to his own projected conduct. He rehearses what he is going to do and inwardly responds to himself. If the response he gets is unsatisfactory, he tries again, until an act is sketched out which calls forth in himself the reflection of the satisfactory response which he hopes to elicit from the real other outside him. Then he can make a gesture which is meaningful in the sense that it is calculated to produce the desired effect.

Among the 'gestures' he makes is speech. This has the peculiar property that it is audible to the speaker as well as to the person to whom he is speaking. Thus he is able to respond to himself with the expected response of 'the other' more easily than is the case with other bodily gestures. 'The vocal gesture,' says Mead, 'has an importance which no other gesture has.' To make Mead's point a little clearer, let us consider an example which he himself uses. 'The meaning of what we are saying,' he says, 'is the tendency to respond to it. You ask someone to bring a visitor a chair. You arouse the tendency to get the chair in the other, but if he is slow to act you get the chair yourself. The response to the vocal gesture is the doing of a certain thing, and you arouse that same tendency in yourself. You are always replying to yourself, just as other people reply.' This means that at least two interrelated processes occur in the mind: the intention and the adumbrated response to the intention; the desire for a chair, expressed as 'Get the chair, please,' *and* the adumbrated chair-getting response that one hopes to elicit, and that *may*, as in Mead's example, spill over into actual overt behaviour, as so often happens with an impatient teacher.

And now Mead takes a further step. Supposing you are playing a game, such as football, in which several people, your side and your opponents, are engaged at the same time. You have the ball at your feet. You must not take account only of one other person, as you may in tennis when you place the ball. In the football situation you have to kick the ball in such a way as to elicit one sort of response from the man to whom you are passing, others from members of your side, and others from members of the opposing team. You must take into yourself a general complicated reflection of the responses of all or many of the others who are implicated, in order to guide your action. This Mead calls the 'generalized other'. What a person does in such a situation is in Mead's words 'controlled by his being everyone else in that team, at least in so far as those attitudes affect his own particular response. We get then an "other" which is an organization of the attitudes of those involved in the same process.' This, in his view, is what happens in the course of socialization. 'The attitude of the generalized other is the attitude of the whole community.'

This split or reflexive interchange in us is, according to Mead, responsible for the emergence of the distinction between 'I' and 'me'. For him the 'me' is the organized set of attitudes which 'me' himself assumes; it is in fact a kind of generalized repository of 'others'. Complicated though his idea is, it is perhaps not quite complicated enough. 'I' is the initiator, the proposer of action, according to Mead, uncalculable and spontaneous. 'I' proposes: 'I shall tell him he's a liar', 'me' responds: 'Liar yourself!' or adumbrates a blow or a turning away in defensive disgust, according to 'me's' version of the 'other'. This may cause 'I' to change his tune and make another proposal. Control of 'I' is established by the internalized 'other', which may be an individual 'other' or an organized deposit representing society such as 'me' represents it. But something else is there too. In the conversation between 'I' and the internalized other, if conversation it can be called, 'I' comes to recognize that the response is made to him. The generalized other says: 'If *you* do this then *you* will get black looks.' The adumbrated response of the 'other' inside the total self generates the idea of a 'me' to which the response is directed. Thus three elements get differentiated: the 'I', the responding set of attitudes deposited by 'others' (which Mead identifies with the 'me'), and a 'me' whose conduct is being internally criticized.

It will be seen that Mead's account is not unlike the tripartite analysis of the self proposed by the psycho-analysts. The 'generalized' other is like the 'super-ego', while Mead's spontaneous 'I' is like the psycho-analysts' 'id'. The 'me' is certainly not like the psycho-analysts' 'ego', but that is because the two systems were constructed for different purposes.

Mead's curious formulation of the problem has been dealt with in some detail, partly because he is the only person who has ever made an attempt to account for the emergence of self-consciousness, and partly because, however fanciful one may think his account to be, it throws a light on those internal conversations with ourselves which constitute a great deal of our thinking and it registers the importance of social intercourse in developing not only the idea of ourselves as separate beings but also as beings with standards of conduct incorporated from the people with whom we have had to deal. As Kingsley Davis[6] puts it: 'No sharp line can be drawn between our own selves and the selves of others, since our own selves function in our experience only in so far as the selves of others function in our experience also.'

Furthermore, once the idea of 'me' is born, I become not only aware of myself, but an object of value to myself. To quote Kingsley Davis once more: 'Since it is built out of the attitudes of others, the self cannot help but place a value on these attitudes apart from or in spite of organic satisfaction. This is especially true of one kind of attitude – the attitude of approval and disapproval; for this offers a key to much else. It is only through the approval of others that the self can tolerate the self.'[7]

Lest it should be thought that too much stress has been laid on the part played by society in turning an infant into a human being, let us glance at cases where social influence has been absent. Davis had the opportunity of examining two girls, both of them illegitimate and both confined to some upper chamber and merely kept alive by being given the minimum of food required for that purpose. At six years of age, Anna could not talk, walk, or do anything that showed intelligence, nor could Isabelle, who was of the same age and had been shut up in the dark with her deaf and dumb mother. Her behaviour was like that of a child of six months. They thought she, too, was deaf, but she wasn't, and after careful teaching she was eventually able to go to school as a normal child. Anna died when she was about 10 and did not enjoy the expert attention that Isabelle received, but all the same she was able to learn to do a few simple tasks. The interesting thing about Isabelle was the rapidity with which she learnt under expert guidance. However that may be, it is quite clear that when these children were found at the age of 6 they could not be described as 'normal human children' – or even as human at all, save in bodily form.

There is for instance the case of two children in India alleged to have been brought up, like Romulus and Remus, by a wolf. They were brought by the villagers to the local clergyman who proceeded to do his best to turn them from naked animals crawling on all fours into human beings. One of them died shortly after capture, the other survived and responded to training by the usual devices of reward and punishment. She acquired the official range of inhibitions, but at the age of seventeen she could utter no more than fifty words.[8]

Then there is the 'wild boy of Aveyron' found in 1800 by hunters. He, too, was but an animal. A local doctor brought him up. He, too, learned to accommodate himself to human requirements, but scarcely learned to talk.

The 'Nuremberg Boy' appeared out of the blue – more correctly, it appears, out of a dungeon – in 1828. He had been deprived of human society, but may have learned to talk when a child. He recovered this particular social skill when he resumed intercourse with other people. His case would seem to indicate the need for persistent social intercourse if human characteristics are to be preserved.

Suppose, then, we agree with Mead that 'The self, as that which can be object to itself, is essentially a social structure, and it arises in social experience'. This means that the selves we are are to a great extent the product of our social contacts. It is from society that we get the indispensable tool of language, including those systems of non-vocal gestures which are used for communication by deaf-mutes. It is from society that we get most of our interests because society provides us with a range of differentially valued activities in which we are invited to participate. It is from society that we acquire our basic moral standards; they can come from nowhere else. Thus a child brought up among the Eskimo, the Samoans, the Chinese, the English, or the Hopi Indians will have a personality appropriate to the culture in which he has been nurtured. The concept of 'human nature' has dwindled to a few basic biological needs and a large range of potentialities one selection of which is cultivated by one society, another by another.

This should make us pause to reflect when the educationalists speak about the 'full development of the personality' as being the aim of education, more especially when some of them advocate extreme permissiveness. They speak as though there were in each of us a little seed called the 'personality' which must be carefully tended and allowed the maximum freedom for it to grow. Nothing could be more mistaken. A permissive social environment shapes and produces one sort of personality, an authoritarian one produces another. Permission is not the *removal* of social influence so that the 'natural' personality can have a chance to develop; it merely replaces one kind of social influence for another. In any case not all the capacities of a person can develop without conflicting with others. Competition conflicts with co-operation and aggressiveness conflicts with pacific attitudes to all mankind. Some societies, such as capitalist ones and the Bedouin Arabs, cultivate competition and aggressiveness, others cultivate co-operation and pacifism. Doubtless all these traits find their place in every society. There is always a certain amount of competition for people's good opinion, for prestige, though we are told that the Zuni Indians are scandalized at any such thing. Aggression may be held justified in self-defence. Co-operation is required for communal tasks, and one must behave pacifically towards one's friends and relations.

All this is true, but societies differ enormously in the stress they lay on the cultivation of one set of qualities, and the degree to which they play down another set. It is not surprising that the Russians insist that they must cultivate a new type of personality to fit in with their way of life. They deprecate the 'individualism' of capitalist countries. We are deeply shocked and tend to say that such a regime stunts the growth of 'the personality'. In fact 'individualism', standing up for oneself, demanding one's rights, seeking one's own advantage, having enterprise, resenting being bossed about and so forth is cultivated by one society, but need not be cultivated in other societies. It is, in fact, required for the efficient running of a capitalist economy. We praise people for standing up for themselves, for 'bettering themselves' through their own efforts and for being different (but not too different) from others. 'Individualism' like all valued human traits is a cultural product. Whether the production of one type of personality is more laudable than the production of another is not our business. The most we can say is that all cultures have their hazards of internal dissension, human misery, and mental disease. If we chose to sit in judgement it is these negative aspects that should claim our attention. If these are reduced to a minimum it is hard to judge whether the type of personality formed by one society is better than the type formed by another.

This emphasis on the part played by society in the production of human beings might lead one to suppose that we are making them out to be mere reflections of the expectations of others, chameleons who change their colour automatically with every change in social setting, responsive to every change of climate.

This is quite clearly not the case. Once the self starts developing a hard central core comes into being, and, indeed, grows harder as the years go by.

To begin with each infant has its own innate set of potentialities, and receives the impact of society in his own particular way, and in the particular form provided by the particular adults and age-mates with whom he comes into contact. They, in turn, are each of them unique because of their specific innate equipment and the specific impact which society has had on them. The notion of the 'society' moulding the personality is a highly abstract one. In fact societies are made up of millions of unique individuals, similar only in that they share certain standards of behaviour. Even identical twins differ because they are not treated exactly alike by the same people, and because they soon interact with different people.

Secondly, each individual has his own biological needs for food, drink, protection, and sexual satisfaction, and the desire to satisfy these, or to acquire the means for their satisfaction, frequently conflicts with the demands of the 'generalized other', and therefore with other parts of himself in so far as he has internalized the social rules.

Thirdly, once the organization of the self has got going it proceeds under integrative principles of its own. We may incorporate a number of relatively independent sets of standards, professional standards, family-life standards, good-fellowship standards, and so on, but there are limits to the inconsistencies we can tolerate. If, therefore, having acquired one set of standards, we are brought into relationship with a group which has a different set, we do not usually accept the new set without a struggle. The advantages of conformity with the new standards may be such as to induce us to re-shuffle our old set, not without appropriate feelings of guilt. On the other hand we may reject the new standards because they do not fit with those we already have. The extent to which we take the one line or the other may be partly due to the type of culture in which we have been bred. If we have been brought up in a culture which phrases moral conduct as a matter of individual responsibility, a culture which cultivates differences of opinion, and gives approval to those who stand out against group pressure even though the approving agent may be on the side of the group, we are more likely to acquire a nonconforming streak. If, on the other hand, we are brought up in a relatively large group of adults all of whom we must indifferently please, or if good-behaviour is phrased constantly in terms of what other people will say, or what the official line is, then the standards of the group have a much greater pull, unless the group is one which is offici-ally condemned – as bourgeois or communist as the case may be. Riesman[9] has suggested that in America there is a move away from the former type of moral standard towards the latter, or 'other-regarding' type, as he calls it.

Fourthly, when we can reflect upon ourselves, we become possessed of a cherished object, as has already been said. This means that we are not only aware of the standards of the groups which we join, we are also liable to ask whether we are getting our dues, whether we have the prestige we think ourselves to merit, whether we are enhancing or debasing ourselves. We not only search the eyes of our fellow members whispering: 'How am I doing?', we also look at ourselves and say: 'What do they think of you? Do you stand high or low?' If the answers conflict, as they frequently do, if the group tolerates us because we conform but rates us low all the same, a conflict is in sight.

Fifthly, and finally, we have the power of reasoning. We not only acquire standards, we reflect upon them. We may expand the social minimum of respect for others to a determination to devote ourselves to the welfare of our fellow men. We may contrast the rules we have acquired with more permissive rules which would allow us a greater range of personal pleasure, and choose the latter. Undoubtedly social intercourse will play its part in present-ing the framework in which such choices can be made, and in presenting alternative choices. No one can think up a code of personal morality entirely and absolutely different from that of the culture in which he has been brought up. All the same it would be idle to deny the influence of reason and reflection, however rare its occurrence – rarer, perhaps, than we like to think.

All this means that although the self-conscious personality is a social product, although its tasks and standards are derived from society, once formed it assumes a certain independence, which frequently brings it into conflict with the groups in which it finds itself. And this is true of *everyone*. It is difficult to express oneself without conjuring up the idea of an individual, with his acquired equipment of standards, interests, and attitudes towards himself, being confronted with a group of undifferentiated members, like going into an empty room impregnated with a pungent odour and shining with bright paint. *Every* member is individualized. The unity of the group lies in the sharing of its purposes, its standards, and the awareness of its very existence, but every individual has other standards, other purposes, and is a member of other groups as well. There is therefore the danger of conflict. The other members may frustrate the acquired demands of any one member, and the very fact of the interdependence of them all means that each is, to a certain extent, at the mercy of the others.

In spite, however, of this acquisition of individual independence, very few people are completely indifferent to group atmosphere. On occasion one may find a person quite completely indifferent to the attitudes of other members of a group, but of such a one we should most likely say that he was 'in' the group but not 'of' it. This, of course, is quite different from standing up against the group on occasion. In such cases the group positively lends vigour to the individual who rejects it, and frequently heat as well. More often, as we shall see when we come to the experimental evidence on the working and structure of groups, people are, even if ever so slightly, ever so superficially, drawn into conformity.

In fact the atmospheres of groups may so change our conduct that we come to doubt that unity of the self of which we hear so much. This is illustrated by a celebrated experiment carried out by Lippitt and White,[10] followers of the topological school of Kurt Lewin. Four small groups of eleven-year-old boys were subjected to three different régimes: an 'authoritarian' régime in which the adult leader of the group ordered them about and told them what to do, a 'democratic' régime in which he consulted them and discussed their problems with them, and a *'laissez-faire'* régime where the leader left them to their own devices. The same leaders put on these different 'acts' in turn and each group was subjected to each type of régime. One group was rebellious under authority, the others were cowed into apathy, but let themselves go under the other two more permissive climates. All groups were industrious and well-knit under the democratic régime, while under *laissez-faire* they were rather frustrated and bewildered, not knowing quite what to do. There were several complications introduced: the leaders left the room for a period, and it was noted that those undergoing democratic 'treatment' went on working, while those enjoying the temporary release from authoritarianism did nothing; the visit of a 'stranger', who criticized their work, had a different effect in each climate.

The relevance of this experiment in our present context is that the same boys behaved quite differently in each social situation. If an observer had seen them only in one situation he would have given an entirely different account of their 'personalities' from that which would be given by someone who had seen them in one of the others. This, after all, is in accord with everyday experience. It often happens that two people disagree about the character of a third because each of them has met him or her in different social situations: a mute in one, a chatterbox in the other. Of course, people differ in their responsiveness to different social climates, or, *per contra*, in the 'tightness' of their own organizations, but while the acquired independence and stable structure of the individual must not be forgotten, it must, on the other hand, not be over-emphasized.

An incidental finding in the Lippitt and White experiment may be mentioned because it is relevant to what has gone before. They found on questioning the boys that all except one preferred the régime of 'democracy'. It is significant that they were all young Americans, and that the only one who preferred the 'authoritarian' régime was the son of an autocratic military father. No group, as we have said before, operates in a vacuum.

The pressure of the group on the individual is in the direction of conformity. It may be met with compliance or emotional rejection. The reason for this pressure to conform, against which the nonconformist has to fight, is due to the need people have for approval. This used to be ascribed to a 'group instinct', which, of course, explains nothing. An explanation, however, is not far to seek. In the long period of human childhood the child is dependent upon other people for the satisfaction of all its needs. The good-will of the surrounding adults is essential to his welfare. Desire for signs of goodwill then becomes a secondary objective in itself, and this is generalized to the wider social field. The expression of goodwill on the part of others becomes a measure of his own goodness and value. It is true that some people are very selective and measure themselves by the goodwill of their friends. It is also true that a few people are so far indifferent to human approval that they are only satisfied with the imputed approval of supernatural beings, but it is probably true to say that no one is so self-satisfied as to do without the approval of at least one other person. Most people are continually looking into the eyes of others to see the impression they are making. After all, standards are in the first instance derived from other people; their acceptance is the price we pay for the goodwill we need. It is not surprising that we need constant assurance that we have not sacrificed the satisfaction of our own immediate impulses for nothing.

Another factor which lends additional force to the pressure to conform is that in situations in which there is no objective basis for determining the validity of one's judgements – and such situations are common enough – a consensus of judgements expressed by a group helps us to make up our minds, and – this is the main point – relieves us of an uncomfortable feeling of doubt and uncertainty.

Thus nonconformity is always slightly disagreeable, unless the subject-matter is of complete indifference, or unless we have very strong compensating alternative means of getting approval elsewhere.

The influence of society is brought to bear on the child from two main quarters, from the parents and other adults and from other children. The methods employed in both cases are the same: reward and punishment. The parents demand obedience, the other children demand co-operation. In our society the child is in a sense at the mercy of its father and mother, in many other cultures it is cared for by a number of adults, with the result that when rejected by one it can go for consolation to another. We bring children up in terms of 'right' and 'wrong', 'good' and 'bad' behaviour; elsewhere they make more use of ridicule, or simply bodily removal from the scene of improper conduct.

In general, however, in spite of these important variations in the adult world with which the child interacts, and the technique involved, an account of which is beyond the scope of this volume, socialization by the parents involves two things: a certain content of approved and disapproved conduct, and a preparation for meeting the world in which the child will have to live. The content will vary from culture to culture, from sub-culture to sub-culture within the same society, and from family to family, each of which will supply its own version. This, of course, prepares the child for the future, but another and largely unconscious preparation goes on at the same time: the implanting of general attitudes towards other people.

Very broadly speaking, from the child's experience of its parents (which, of course, from some points of view may be misleading) it acquires a set of expectations about the way other people in the future are likely to behave which will determine its own behaviour. It may achieve a general feeling of security and approach other people without fear. On the other hand it may have felt itself to be scurvily treated and look upon other people as potential enemies. It may find itself constantly compared advantageously or disadvantageously with the little boy next door; it may carry a preoccupation with such comparisons into its future life. It may find that it can get what it wants by screaming and expect to get its own way by similar methods in the future – a hope almost bound to lead to disillusionment.

Such are only a handful of possibilities, but they suffice to show the significant differences which affect the harmony of the groups to which, in the future, the child will belong, and which spring from the first group of which he is a member.

So far as other children go, it is some time before the child has much co-operative contact with them. Susan Isaacs,[11] who had a school for very young children, found that solitary play is characteristic of children of 2 and 3 and that only very occasional groupings occurred of children of 4 and 5. 'When a number of young children are brought together in a given space', she writes, 'but left free to play and move about as they wish, they do not at first constitute a *group* in the psychological sense. They behave simply as a number of independent persons' (p. 213). According to her, such ephemeral groups as do come together do so in a spirit of hostility against an outsider, and she goes so far as to say that 'Whenever two or three or more children draw together in feeling or aim sufficiently to create a group, they tend in their drawing together to find an enemy to the group' (p. 250). In her view this is because in order to like one another they have to husband their hostility elsewhere. They may also band together against adults because there is safety in numbers.

There seems to be agreement that it takes time for children to form groups spontaneously, though it must be noted that most of the evidence comes from middle-class American and English children. When, as in Samoa and in the sub-culture of the working-classes, children are very often put in charge of other children but little older than they are, the formation of stable groups may occur at an earlier age.

By the ages of 6 and 7 more stable groups appear – or can appear if space and opportunity are offered. When this happens the social learning which we call 'give and take' begins. A sense of 'justice' may make its experience earlier if we can generalize from Susan Isaacs' report; her children below the age of 6 had a notion of equal shares. Conflict over the possession of a toy could be settled if each was allowed equal turns with it, but in such cases it is the adult who intervenes. It is not, however, only 'give and take' and 'co-operation' that is learnt when children play in groups with one another; a change of attitude towards the very nature of rules seems to come about. In his book on the *Moral Judgment of the Child*,[12] Piaget distinguishes several stages of attitude towards rules, taking as his main example a complicated game of marbles. At first the child simply plays by and for itself (the stage which Piaget calls: ego-centrism), as he grows older he accepts the rules as coming from outside, as precepts that just have to be obeyed. Later on, however, the rules become means of reciprocal accommodation, a necessary convenience without which a game could not be, but modifiable if circumstances require it. This paves the way for the creation of rules for the purpose of playing games. It is, he argues, only through social sophistication that this development comes about.

When the stage has been reached at which children form social groups, whether in the classroom, the playground, or the street, the stage is set for a conflict of principles. The authority of the parents still holds in many régimes of behaviour, but it has a rival in the standards set by friends. In many situations these may be paramount. The result is a somewhat confused competition of allegiances which is perhaps responsible for the finding of Hartshorn and May[13] in their study of children's morality that: 'The average child of grades 5 to 8 (10–13 years) is chiefly a creature of circumstance. Whether his conduct happens to be good or bad, it is ethically unorganized.' They insist on the importance of the situation when judging or predicting a child's honesty and helpfulness.

In general as time goes on during adolescence there is a decline in the reliance on parents, an increase in assertion of individual independence, a greater reliance on the judgement of age-mates and an increase in awareness of extenuating circumstances and special factors when making moral judgements. Dr J. F. Morris[14] in a study of value-judgements in adolescents ranging in age from 11 to 18 found that among his English subjects 'with the decline of reliance on authority comes the judgement that one should not lean too heavily upon friends'. The American literature leads one to suppose that there, at any rate, the judgement of coevals assumes an importance which ousts parental authority. This minor conflict of evidence is significant. The importance of 'teen-agers' in America, due perhaps to the well-known ambiguous position of immigrants, and the way in which 'teen-age' culture is systematically cultivated by parents, commerce, and the 'teen-agers' themselves, should put us on our guard when we generalize from the results of American research to corresponding groups in our own society. This point is reinforced by another American finding. Eugene Lerner[15] compared the moral judgement of children between 6 and 12 belonging to two status groups in an American city. According to him high status parents employ fewer coercive techniques of control and their children are not so prone to see principles as external and unvarying (Piaget's second stage) as is the case with children of low status parents, while another investigator, D. MacRae,[16] found that low status children tended more often to support friends against parents and teachers, when this was an issue, so that they might be said to be more emotionally mature. Whether such particular differences could be found in Great Britain if we compared children from different classes, it is impossible to say: perhaps the reverse might be the case; but at any rate we learn that it is risky to generalize even within one society from material collected in one class to members of another. The significance of the 'peer' group is discussed further in Chapter 9.

Behaviour in groups is thus determined by the general cultural standards assimilated by the participants, by their innate and acquired individual characteristics, by the demands of the subgroup in which the persons are acting, and by the particular situation that confronts them. In the case of any individual, sometimes one of these factors will be dominant, and sometimes another.

CHAPTER 3

THE STUDY OF SMALL GROUPS

In this chapter five approaches to the study of small groups will be discussed, two of them very briefly and the other three at rather greater length.

Observation. It might be argued with unanswerable cogency that all methods of scientific inquiry involve observation. Of course they do. The point of including it here is to contrast cases in which observation of 'real life' situations is the method adopted, with cases in which some kind of experimental control is used. In social-psychological research into life in a village, a factory, a housing estate, or a hospital the whole point is to find out what is happening with the minimum disturbance introduced by the investigator. He must disturb the situation somehow by his questioning, interviewing, and form-filling, but this can be reduced by what is sometimes called 'participant observation' when he makes some attempt at melting into the scene by becoming a factory hand, a resident, or a nurse.

The position of the social scientist in the process of observing is frequently discussed. It is complained that he has no accepted role except the invidious one of 'snooper'. In America people seem to be more amenable to being watched and investigated than they are in Britain, where the social scientist is liable to be suspect. This means that elaborate precautions have to be taken beforehand, and the prestige of any parties who are likely to be ruffled if they are not told beforehand must be safeguarded; the conflicting interests of industrialists and Trade Unionists must be considered when research of this kind is carried out in the industrial field; the suspicions of operatives and housewives must be lulled to rest; the goodwill of all officials must be delicately courted. Professor Simey has put the problem as one of 'getting in, staying in, and getting out'. Once the observer has 'got in', he must obviously win such confidence as will enable him to stay there. This is clearly more easy when the subject of his research is connected with an issue, such as housing or easing difficult human relations, which the subjects of his research have at heart. It is harder when they are quite mystified by the questions they are asked. Because of this, a little subterfuge is not unknown here and there. On the other hand, if the matter of inquiry is one of burning interest, or if the subjects of the inquiry have become themselves interested in the research, can the social scientist just snap his files together when he has got all the information he wants, and march off? The subjects may feel that they have been led up the garden path, betrayed, used as guinea-pigs, and so forth. Extraction from the scene of investigation for the sensitive scientist is often a delicate matter, particularly when he remembers that the reputation of his subject, which anyway is rather dubious, is at stake.

With all these difficulties it is not surprising that so much social research centres round school-children and criminals; both categories of person are accessible and neither is likely to complain.

Experiment. The function of experiment in scientific research is to produce a controlled situation in which the factors thought to be relevant to the effect which is being investigated can be varied in turn, the others being kept constant. By this means the influence of each variable can be studied, and the results generalized to apply to situations outside the laboratory. In the physical sciences the problem is fairly straightforward, though the technique employed may be extremely complicated. The material with which the physical scientist is dealing does not resist manipulation, though it may be difficult to manipulate, it does not change its nature in the presence of the experimenter himself, and he, in turn, can be pretty certain that the phenomena he studies in his laboratory are no different from the phenomena outside in the real world. The social scientist is in a very different position. In human behaviour we know that intellectual ability, mood, personal background, and personal aims and interests are all relevant, and that everyone is different from everyone else; the complete control of all relevant factors is impossible. To get round this you may have to use a large number of subjects or groups, and repeat the experiment a number of times, in the hope that personal and ephemeral differences will cancel out.

Again, there are limits to what you can do to human beings in laboratories. For your experiment to be a success there must be some co-operation on the part of your subjects. They must be prepared to place themselves at your disposal, it may be for hours at a time, and though American students of psychology seem to be the most amenable of persons, even their patience is exhaustible. Finally the social psychologist is awkwardly placed when he tries to generalize from the results he has obtained in his laboratory to 'real life' situations. It is not easy to imitate 'real life' in a laboratory; the motives engendered are never quite the same as those operating in the relevant 'real-life' situation; the things the subjects are invited to do may be boring, and their participation only sustained by goodwill, whereas you may want to apply your findings to situations in which passions may be roused. In a laboratory you want to separate out factors you believe to be important in human social situations in general; your experiment may therefore be of an extremely simple character and tedious to take part in for that very reason. You may want to find out how people's work varies with the presence of an audience. You get your subject to do endless sums by himself, and then in the presence of witnesses. What could be more dreary? And yet something of interest emerges, as we shall see, even from this apparently trivial inquiry.

However, in spite of these obstacles experimental social psychologists, particularly in America, have shown considerable ingenuity, and some of their experiments will be referred to in Chapters 8 and 9. As an example of ingenuity let us take two experiments carried out in America. The problem in both was much the same: the creation of a prestige hierarchy. In everyday life you have, in almost every group, some people who have greater prestige than others, and the communication between them is often fraught with difficulty. Are there any general principles which apply in such situations, even though such principles may appear in a different guise from one case to another? You cannot very well watch real-life situations because they are too complicated, and you may not know what to look for. In a laboratory, on the other hand, if you can establish a hierarchy artificially, you may be able to introduce variations which you cannot introduce in real life and see what happens.

Harold H. Kelley[1] got together a number of students and divided them into smaller groups of eight. The smaller groups were told that they, in turn, would be subdivided and put in different rooms and that one sub-group would be given a pattern of rectangles, while the other group would be given a collection of bricks. The first group was to communicate with the second, telling them how to lay the bricks out so as to correspond with their pattern. The communications were to be written and sent through the experimenter. Neither of the sub-groups knew which of them was to send messages and which to lay the bricks. In point of fact both sub-groups did exactly the same – they laid bricks in response to prearranged instructions purporting to come from the other room, but really coming from the experimenter. The bricklayers were also told that they could communicate with the people who were supposed to be giving them instructions. It was these communications which formed the data of the experiment.

After being told the general plan of the experiment as it was to be conceived by them, the two sub-groups were taken away and given further information. One sub-group would be told that their task of bricklaying was extremely difficult, requiring considerable skill in interpreting the instructions; as for the instructions, the sub-group that sent them out (supposedly) had a very menial and humdrum task. The other sub-group would be told that the really difficult thing to do was to give adequate instructions from a distance, the task of the bricklayers was routine – simply following instructions. They had the most menial task. This seemed to work. The sub-group who were told how important their job was felt themselves to be a cut above the other sub-group who, they imagined, simply had the dull job of sending messages; those who were told that their job was of very little importance or difficulty, felt themselves inferior to their friends in the other room who had the fascinating and difficult job of devising appropriate instructions. Kelley introduced a further complication. Some of the groups were told that they might move 'up' or 'down' as the experiment proceeded, others were told that this would be impossible in the interest of the results. Finally there were control groups who were told that the two tasks of brick-laying and giving instructions were equally important. The material collected, which consisted of messages to the (supposed) instructors, showed marked differences according to whether they were sent by 'Low Status' or 'High Status' groups, and also according to whether the groups thought themselves to be mobile or not. Some of the results will be mentioned in Chapter 8.

The other exercise in the construction of prestige groups was somewhat simpler. John Thibaut[2] exploited the fact that some games which children play involve two roles, an active and a subservient one. His subjects were boys from settlement homes and summer camps in Boston, and he had altogether 10 or 12 boys which he divided into two teams. He made use of three games; in one of them one team had to form human arches for the others to run under, in another they had to form a human chain for the others to run up against, while in the third they had to hold targets at which bean-bags were thrown, and then they had to retrieve the bags. These are all obviously of lower status than the active roles which the other team played. The games were played four times, but variations were introduced. The experimenter treated the 'low-status' team coldly and unsympathetically, while the 'high-status' team were praised for their prowess. In the interval between the rounds a planted observer egged the 'low-status' team on to rebel, to demand a change; in some cases this was disallowed, thereby increasing the frustration of the unhappy menials, in some cases it was allowed. All this was contrasted with yet other cases in which the two teams changed round. One is happy to read that after persistent frustration in the first of these treatments the wretched 'low-status' boys were given their fling.

The purpose of this was not so much to investigate communication as to study group-cohesion in the low-status groups. Again, we shall refer to the findings in another chapter.

These two examples may serve as instances of social psychological experimentation.

A final warning must be added. The results of many, perhaps most, experiments will be bound to seem rather trivial. This is only natural, because after all we have been living in groups all over the world for many thousands of years, and every living adult has accumulated a good deal of experience in his one life-time about the behaviour of his fellow-men. The result is that psychological experimentation rarely results in discoveries; at best it calls attention to unfamiliar aspects of behaviour which are only half-noticed, but which, when pointed out, are easily recog-nized. To condemn experimentation on this score is to miss the point of the process altogether. As we have said, the experimenter is trying to disentangle, and, so far as he can, to measure the factors involved in social interaction, however familiar they may be to common sense. When he has done this, and indeed in the process of doing it, he aims at constructing a deductive theoretical system by means of which, from a relatively small number of assumptions, the whole range of human interaction will be ex-plained. This may seem a tall order, and its achievement certainly lies in the future, but until it is achieved social psychology will remain an immature science. In any case, the hunches and in-tuitions of common sense, however justified they may turn out to be, will never satisfy the social scientist until he has verified and refined them by patient investigation.

Sociometry. The technique of sociometric assessment was in-vented by Dr J. L. Moreno.[3] Groups vary in their cohesiveness, and every group has what might be called a 'preference structure', a network of likes, dislikes, and indifferences which links its mem-bers to one another. This, of course, is familiar enough, but mere observation only enables us to detect friendships, cliques, antag-onism, and indifferences in a very rough and ready way. Investi-gators have, to be sure, watched groups of children playing and noted how often Johnny speaks to Billy, and spurns the advances of little Horace. The sociometric approach is different. The par-ticipants of the group situation are simply asked whom they would like to sit next, work with, share a room with, or spend their leisure time with, and so on. The 'criterion', as it is called, must be specific. 'Whom do you like best?' will not do. They may be given one choice or several choices, and then the sociometric status is calculated for each by totting up the number of preferences each receives. The sociometric structure of the whole group for any criterion can also be represented diagrammatically with lines joining the chooser to the person or persons of his choice, and, if the question has been asked, lines distinguishable from the others joining the hostile to the objects of their animosity. By this means pairs, chosen by no one but each other, cliques of friends, chains of friendship, popular stars and unchosen 'isolates' can be revealed, and close-knit companions stand out in contrast to the pitiful 'neglectees'.

This method of assessment is used, as will appear later on, for a variety of purposes. Moreno himself, and his associates, used it in the New York State Training School for Girls. They lived in houses presided over by a 'house-mother', and it was found, as one might expect, that some houses were more harmonious than others. This became clearer when sociometric assessments were made, and these enabled the organizers to reshuffle the inhabitants so that every girl was in a group which provided her with some kind of friendly companionship. Such a use of the method might be called 'therapeutic', because it is held with some reason that people are frustrated and miserable when they are constantly with people who reject them. The technique is also used as a basis for putting children who like one another to sit next one another in class, and for putting workmen who like one another to work together, for much the same reason.

It is also used as a measure of cohesion in groups. It is argued that if you have sub-groups within a large collectivity, such as a school, a camp, a service unit, or a factory, such that choices on any criterion may fall within the group or outside it, then a group in which the majority of the choices are directed to the group members and not outside is more cohesive than one in which the opposite occurs. A well-known instance of this is the comparison between two air-crews in the United States Air Force. One of them was said to have low morale, the other high morale. In the latter case nearly all the choices on the criterion: Whom would you like to fly with? were directed to members of the crew, many of them being directed to the senior officers. In the former case, on the other hand, there were small cliques in the crew, but most of the choices went outside and none of them went to the senior officers, who were, indeed, named on criterion: 'With whom would you not like to fly?'

Yet another use is made by experimentalists. If an experiment, such as that of Thibaut already mentioned, is concerned with altering patterns of friendship under changed conditions, it is important at the outset to see what the initial pattern of friendship is. Thibaut, for instance, divided his groups into teams in such a way that no difference existed in the mutual attractions within each team at the outset of the experiment. When the experiment is ended a further assessment is made to see whether a difference has been made.

Mustapha Sherif, for example,[4] wanted to study sub-groups in the making. He took a number of boys to a camp in a large camping area. After discovering by a sociometric test who was friendly with whom, he divided the whole group into two sub-groups, separating friends so far as he could. He then told each sub-group to go off to different parts of the camping area, to build themselves some kind of a gang centre. They took to this, as one might well imagine, and soon the 'Red Devils' and the 'Bull-Dogs' were two competing teams. They were pitted against one another in games, and by various devices of a dubious ethical character, hostility was worked up between them. It is not surprising that in the post-experimental sociometric assessment, the members of the two teams chose one another rather than their erstwhile friends if they happened to be in the other group.

We shall meet with several experiments later in which sociometric status is used as a measuring rod.

Field Theory and Topology.[5] This is not a technique of inquiry so much as a conceptual system, a way of looking at social interaction. Kurt Lewin was the founder of a school of social psychological theory, which is now largely concentrated in the Research Centre for Group Dynamics at the Massachusetts Institute of Technology, and is associated with the names of Bavelas, Cartwright, French, Festinger, Lippitt, and many others, whose researches will be discussed in the following chapters. Lewin was originally a member of the *Gestalt* group in Germany, and, like many of his colleagues, was trained in the physical sciences. This may well be the reason why he views social situations in terms of fields of force, much as the electrical engineer may think in terms of magnetic fields. It is impossible to give a complete account of the details of the 'Field Theory', but a brief résumé of its more important features is necessary because it has inspired so much social-psychological research, the reports of which are not easy to understand unless the reader has some knowledge of the conceptual framework – and, indeed, the jargon – of the writers.

A fundamental concept is that of 'life-space'. Lewis deprecated the common-sensical notion of the individual with his equipment of 'instincts', 'desires', 'motives', or whatever dynamic engines may be imputed to him, acting in an indifferent environment. We ought to think of the individual and the environment as constituting a whole interrelated system. The life-space consists of the individual person at a particular moment of time in a setting partly determined by the physical objects present, partly by his interpretation of them, how he perceives them, their significance for him at that moment. It is also coloured by what Wright and Barker[6] call the 'behaviour setting'. By this they mean certain culturally coercive pressures which make certain behaviour appropriate and other behaviour inappropriate, as is the case with a sewing party at the rectory, a school class, discussion, or the nineteenth hole on a golf links. It may be further complicated by 'unreal' as well as 'real' elements, hopes, ambitions, fears and so on.

It must be admitted that 'life-space' is used in a very general sense. It may be restricted to what is actually present here and now, what one can see, hear, and touch, or it may have a wide reference and include that which is not actually present but which comes within the scope of planning for the relatively immediate future, such as the theatre one might visit, the friend one might call upon, or the solution one seeks to a problem, and the region through which one must pass in order to reach these objectives, whether geographical or steps in a process of reasoning.

In the individual there are certain tensions demanding release. Because of these the life-space achieves dynamic vitality. Forces push the individual towards goals, and increase as the goal is approached; the objectives, whether physical or 'mental', such as the solution of a problem, are said to acquire positive 'valence', and the person is said to 'locomote' in their direction. On the other hand the position in which the person now is acquires 'negative valence' and there is a force pushing him out of it. He may not know how to assuage his tensions, in which case he makes trial-and-error random 'locomotions'.

But there are not only goals, there are also barriers, with 'negative valence' and forces pushing away from them. What the person will do depends on the relative strengths of the forces pushing him in various directions. Thus it is obvious that the 'life-space' is constantly changed with 'locomotion', and also with changing awareness, in which case it is often said to be 'restructured'. Supposing you perceive a goal attainable across a field, the field has 'positive valence' as a region leading to the goal. When, however, you become aware that the field forms an intimate part of the life-space of a dangerous bull, your own life-space is quickly restructured and the field acquires the negative valence of a barrier.

This pictorial representation of the person in a life-space, which, as we have seen, may be purely 'psychological', as in problem solution, or psychologically interpreted, as in all situations in which we act, in the ordinary sense of the word, tempted Lewin to develop a kind of geometry of life-spaces, and he drew analogies for this purpose from the branch of mathematics called 'Topology'. This does not really amount to very much, and it must be confessed that 'psychological topology' does not bear any close relationship to the mathematical calculations of the same name. It merely serves to represent paths of 'locomotion' and barriers in a vivid and unusual way. We see, for instance, the significance of a totally encompassing boundary when we think of a situation in which a child is required to do something unpleasant on pain of punishment if he refuses. The task has repelling negative valence, pushing him towards the alternative, which also has negative valence pushing him back to the task. Two forces equal and opposite to one another will drive the child from the field – a concept much used by the 'field theorists'. You must, therefore, stop up all the gaps of escape by enclosing the child in a barrier from which no escape is possible: he may be enclosed literally in a room, or taught about the all-seeing eye of God. The latter is found to be both effective and inexpensive.

A further complication of the life-space is introduced by the concept of 'induced' forces. These are forces exercised in the main by other people in authority, or by groups to which a person belongs; they do not spring from the person himself, but from his relation to others. In the Lewin, Lippitt, and White experiment in social climates described on page 32 the leader in the authoritarian régime was the origin of an 'induced' force which kept the boys busy while he was in the room; when he was away the children abandoned their tasks. If the 'induced' force is not consonant with the 'own' force of the subject, it ceases to operate when its origin (leader, foreman, etc.) is withdrawn; if it is consonant with the 'own' force of the subject it may be added to it; and this increase of energy may be maintained without the pressure of the leader himself. The behaviour of mice in the absence of cats has achieved a scientific status.

All this is concerned with individual behaviour, and Lewin has much to say about the structure of the personality into which we need not go. Turning now to group psychology, we shall expect the group to be conceived as a field of force not identical with the mere sum of the 'tension systems' which make it up. We have already considered an experiment to show how different group fields will affect the same people. The group, in fact, may under certain circumstances be thought of as an entity 'locomoting' towards a goal, with variations in the distribution of forces as it approaches it, or as the goal recedes. From what has been said already we shall not be surprised to find the field theorists defining the cohesion of the group as 'the total field of forces which act on the members to remain in the group'.[7] These may be variously distributed, there may be some very keen members, and others less keen; the important members may be keener than the others but 'induce' them to remain. The forces may be enjoyment of the company of the group, the prestige of the group, or the need of the group as a means towards an end which cannot be achieved without their co-operation, whether the desired end be the immediate result of group action or some indirect result such as a wage-packet.

One way of conceiving the field of force in a group is to think of its state throughout a period of time as a condition of 'quasi-stationary equilibrium'. A group attitude, or rate of output, is the resultant of forces operating in opposite directions and reaching some point of equilibrium. A level of prejudice against, say, for-eigners is the resultant of forces favourable towards foreigners (humanitarian, etc.) and forces against them (e.g. threat of losing employment). In order to change the situation in the group, the forces must be changed. Again, to raise the accepted level of out-put the forces which favour work must be raised or forces which are antagonistic to work must be lowered, or both. Raising the forces towards higher output without lowering the forces against it is likely to lead to an increase in tension; lowering the forces against a given amount of output and thus releasing forces in favour of it is likely to result in a lowering of tension. Since these forces operate on all the members of the group, and since the individual is subjected to the internal pressure of the group-field, it is clear that any attempt to alter the individual member by him-self will be far less effective than altering the standards of the whole group. The practical importance of this principle will be discussed in Chapter 9.

Somewhat unfortunately Lewin gave quasi-mathematical ex-pressions to his theory. He used a somewhat cumbersome set of symbols to represent forces towards this or that goal and away from this or that barrier. We need not concern ourselves with them; they give a spurious air of mathematical accuracy which is quite unwarranted, and it is noteworthy that a recent well-informed account[8] of Field Theory makes use of none of them.

It will be noted that Field Theory concentrates on the situ-ation. The past of the participants is not neglected, but treated differently. In infancy, for instance, a child may have acquired a fear of authority because of the relations between himself and his father. Sophisticated common-sense, influenced by psycho-analytic thought, will endow him with a 'complex', a fixed, hard, little knot of attitudes which remains with him all his life unless it is untied by skilful therapeutic hands. It will make itself felt on appropriate occasions, and we shall say: 'He acts as he does be-cause of his complex about authority'. Such a way of looking at the matter is rejected by the field theorists. They will not deny the significance of the child's relations with his father, but they will insist that we ought rather to follow up its precise effects from situation to situation, if we are interested in the life history of the child. The present situation contains in potentiality the resultant of all the situations through which the individual has passed, and what will happen *now* will be the resultant of all the forces in the field at this moment. This clearly allows for considerable flexibility of conduct. It is a valuable correction to those theories which are concerned with the individual in independence of his environment, whether physical or social. The field theorists call attention to the variety of human behaviour in different contexts; those who are mainly concerned with the individual apart from his environment stress the uniformity of his conduct. Doubtless both approaches have their merits, but for group-psychology a concentration on the situation here and now as it unfolds itself is essential.

George C. Homans. Without doubt the most illuminating book on group-psychology published in the last few years is *The Human Group*[9] by Professor George C. Homans of Harvard University. Like the work of Lewin and his followers, it is important for its contribution to social-psychological theory. In it Homans expounds a framework of hypotheses intended to co-ordinate the phenomena of group activity. It has the great merit of being enjoyable to read and free of the distressing jargon which mars so much of the American literature on the subject. It is to be hoped that a brief account of his theoretical views, which cannot possibly do justice to his book, will encourage readers to go to the original.

Homans subjects the reports of five groups of very different natures, written by other people, to theoretical analysis. The five groups are: the bank-wiring group in the Hawthorn Works of the Western Electric Company in Chicago; the Norton Street Gang, described by W. F. Whyte; the family as found in the Polynesian island of Tikopia, described by Raymond Firth; 'Hilltown', a small town in New England, whose disintegration was described by D. H. Hatch; and the 'Electrical Equipment

Company', an industrial organization suffering from certain internal conflicts which was investigated by C. M. Arensberg and D. Macgregor. The first three may be said to constitute positive evidence, and the last two negative evidence: what happens when the factors Homans believes to be important are not present.

The bank-wiring group is used as a kind of paradigm, and something must be said about it for those not already familiar with the much publicized 'Hawthorn Experiment'. There were nine wiremen, working in a room, wiring telephone equipment. They worked in rows of three, each row behind the other, and were attended by two soldermen and supervised by two supervisors. The ones in front worked on 'connector' equipment, which was paid at a slightly higher rate and conferred prestige; the ones at the back worked on 'selector' equipment, which carried rather less prestige. They were paid by group piece rates, divided into differential shares, so that it was to their interest to raise output as high as possible. In point of fact the output remained extraordinarily constant, and below their actual capacities. This uniform and restricted rate was a controlling agency in the group, giving rise to protests when any individual exceeded it or fell below it.

Homans starts off by saying that groups are formed for a purpose: 'People do not just get together; they get together for a purpose'. There are motives for each member to join a group, there are the activities which the group engages in, and there are the interactions between the members which the activities of the group bring about. These three factors, sentiment (which includes original motives and those derived during the group activities), activity, and interaction are interrelated. If you alter any of them, you will alter the other two, with one possible exception. Every group tends to develop a pyramidal structure, to throw up 'leaders', who are well-thought-of by their followers either because they possess special skills, or because they are popular – and we shall learn the bases of popularity as we go on – or because they are both. In some groups, of course, the pyramidal pattern is consciously established, by the appointment of foremen, officers, bishops, monitors, and so on. Some groups may remain entirely egalitarian, especially friendship groups, but where there is anything specific to be done a leader nearly always emerges spontaneously.

Now every group, if it is to persist, can be thought of as preserving itself in an environment, which provides the condition of the group's activity. Thus, granted that the sentiments which bring the members of the group together in the first place are there, the general scheme of what they have to do – the 'external system', as Homans calls it – is dictated by the nature of their task. The wiring of 'connector' and 'selector' banks demands one sort of action, gang life with its bowling competitions another, and family life on a South Sea island another. This 'external system' of activity dictates the amount and kind of interaction which will take place between the members of the group.

We now come to Homans' first and major hypothesis: 'If the interactions between the members of a group are frequent in the external system, sentiments of liking will grow up between them, and these sentiments will lead in turn to further interactions over and above the interaction of the external system' (p. 112). Furthermore this liking will be increased if there is disliking of outsiders.

The hypothesis that interaction leads to mutual liking may at first sound somewhat extreme. It may be more obvious to Americans than to Englishmen. Homans readily admits that people of very contrasting temperaments may get on one another's nerves, that if one of them is in a position to order other people about he will tend to be rather disliked, and that when a group is in difficulties mutual recrimination may occur and the group may dissolve, though, on the other hand, difficulties may draw them closer together. Apart from these exceptions, however, the hypothesis fits in with common sense, and has been verified by experimental procedure. If we have to deal with other people a lot, we accommodate ourselves to them and they to us, and at the lowest emotional level some kind of feeling of 'getting along together' is engendered.

The importance of the hypothesis, as quoted above, lies in the second half. When the interaction demanded by the external system has established some kind of fellowship among the participants, there will be further interaction *over and above the interaction of the external system*. This constitutes what Homans calls the 'internal system'. The bank-wirers in front interacted more with one another than they did with the ones at the back of the room, and *vice versa*. Therefore two cliques developed. Each clique played games among themselves during the lunch interval; the clique in front was decorous, as befitted their prestige, the ones behind were somewhat loud in their conduct. A mild rivalry developed between the two, the clique at the back tending to do things to irritate the clique in front. They were all, however, united *vis-à-vis* the wiremen working in the main shop.

The external system sets certain norms of conduct for doing the job; the internal system, too, precipitates its norms, among them being the accepted rate of output. Homans accepts the principle we have already enunciated, that groups precipitate their own norms out of the very process of interaction. He quotes with approval Malinowski's words: 'Law and order arise out of the very process which they govern.' The acting out of rules is associated with sentiment, and we come to another important hypothesis: 'The higher the rank of a person within a group, the more nearly his activities conform to the norms of the group', (p. 141) and, it will be found, *vice versa*. This principle clearly limits the range of action of the leader to a large extent, though because he scores high on keeping the major rules, he may be allowed licence when it comes to minor ones. Among the bank-wirers it was the clique in front who kept to the group norms more than the group at the back. In the Norton Street Gang, it was the leaders whose behaviour was close to the standard, low-ranking members tending to deviate more, and thus depress their position further – a point of significance for students of delinquency.

Since interaction leads to consolidation, and consolidation in turn to the establishment of rules of conduct, it is not surprising that when the inhabitants of 'Hilltown' ceased to interact as exclusively as they had in the past, because of the opening up of new communications to the outside world, the standards of conduct collapsed.

Next, we have a hypothesis concerning the interaction between people of unequal rank. The first is to the effect that 'A person of higher social rank than another originates interaction for the latter more often than the latter originates interaction for him' (p.145). This, as we shall see later, is an important consideration for understanding the principles of communication. The second runs: 'When two persons interact with one another, the more frequently one of the two originates interaction for the other, the stronger will be the latter's sentiment of respect (*or hostility*) towards him, and the more nearly will the frequency of interaction be kept to the amount characteristic of the external system' (p. 247). Thus in Tikopia the father is revered by his son, but more intimate with his daughter, on the other hand the son initiates interaction with his maternal uncle as much as the latter does with him; in consequence the relations between the two are affectionate.

This last principle introduces us to the dangers of the position of leadership, which also will occupy our attention in a later chapter.

Finally we have the problem of deviance and social control. 'Control', says Homans, 'is the process by which, if a man departs from his existing degree of obedience to a norm, his behaviour is brought back to that degree'. (p. 301). This does not, of course, mean that there are mechanical methods of ensuring equilibrium for all groups, but rather that if a system is in a state approximating to equilibrium, there will be reactions to deviation calculated to restore it. The problem of equilibrium in groups of all sizes is of burning interest to social psychologists, and Homans introduces the conception of a 'moving equilibrium' in which appropriate compensating alternations are made throughout a system undergoing change – e.g. a firm expanding. The position of a sub-group, such as that of the design engineers in the 'Electric Equipment Company', may be one of central importance and high prestige when the firm is small. When, however, the firm expands, with all the 'line and staff' organization that goes with expansion, the position of the sub-group may change to the discontent of its members. It was this kind of maladjustment that caused the trouble in the 'Electrical Equipment Company' which Arensberg and Macgregor were called upon to investigate. The process of change had, as it were, thrown the organization out of gear.

It will be seen that Homans' approach is by no means incompatible with that of the field theorists. The latter are interested in the forces operating in the actual situations which present themselves in the external and internal systems. What Homans has done is to place these situations in a broader theoretical framework.

It must be emphasized once more that the account given here of Homans' work presents the barest skeleton of his theory; other aspects will be drawn upon in the following pages.

CHAPTER 4

PERMANENT SMALL GROUPS

I: The Family

No classification in the social sciences is ever entirely satisfactory; the material to be classified is too complex and untidy. We may, however, distinguish between three types of small group – or 'primary groups', as Cooley called them – those which cater for many interests and activities, those which are concerned with one interest or type of activity, but which have a certain permanence, and groups actually face-to-face in a particular situation. Under the first heading – the small groups which cater for many interests and activities – we may put the family, the village, and the neighbourhood. Under the second heading – the small groups concerned with one interest or type of activity – we put the club, the smaller units of the services, the working group in industry, the Women's Institute and so on. The difference between these two is fairly obvious. You *live* in the family, the village, or the neighbourhood, and your relations with other people living in the family, village, or neighbourhood are general, in the sense that they are not concerned with any particular aspect of life. You go to the club or Women's Institute for recreation or instruction, you belong to the Services as an occupation or because the law says you have got to, and you belong to your work group because that is the way you earn your living. The family, the village, and the neighbourhood may be said to be 'natural' groups; they come into being out of the process of having and caring for children and living in close proximity to other people. The other groups, in the second category, are specialized; they come into being through the need to form special groups to cater for particular social needs. This is not to say that what happens in such groups is by any means confined to the special purpose for which they come together. As Homans has pointed out, when the 'external' system, which is concerned with the purpose of the group, is established, an 'internal' system of informal relations, personal jealousies, customary ways of doing things, and norms of behaviour will develop.

The third group, which is the subject matter of Chapters 7, 8, and 9, is the actual face-to-face process of a group in a particular situation. This category is distinguished from the other two by different criteria: the criteria of time and space. The groups in the first two categories have a certain permanence. One thinks of their members, not at a particular moment and in the same place at that moment, but as lasting for a considerable period, during which the members are by no means always co-present with one another. Indeed, in the case of the village or the neighbourhood, this may never occur. They are spatially defined, of course, but the members may never meet as a body in one place. Our third category includes such groups as committees, problem-solving groups in laboratories, discussion groups, or groups of people working in the same room at any particular moment. There is, it will be seen, a certain overlap between the third category and the other two. A group called together for experimental purposes is obviously a purely *ad hoc* group, but a working group studied *in situ* for two or three hours may well be a group that constantly works together. As a group *in situ* it comes under our third heading, as a group with a life of its own it comes under the second heading. Moreover what happens when it is observed can only be understood in the light of its accumulated history. Thus it must be admitted that some of the material discussed in later chapters is classifiable under both of these headings.

It is obvious that the third type of group is most easily studied, because you can form 'artificial' groups in the laboratory, set them problems, or subject them to various stimuli, and watch what happens. The result is that we have a great deal of research devoted to this kind of material, which accounts for the amount of space in this book which has been allotted to this subject.

With regard to the second type of group, the most extensive studies have been in the field of industry, and these have been excluded from our consideration because they have been dealt with in this series by J. A. C. Brown in his *The Social Psychology of Industry*.[1]

We come now to the first type of group: the family, the village, and the neighbourhood. Here we are in a difficulty. There is at once too much and too little evidence derived from research. Volumes have been written about the family, there is a good deal of speculation and high-minded theorizing about the neighbourhood, much of which has been contradicted by such research as has been done, while our rural sociology is little short of a disgrace. We have several unpublished pieces of research on rural communities, but unhappily all too few of them get published because they are alleged to have no market value. The situation in America is very different.

In this chapter and the two that follow an attempt will be made to show what aspects of the three groups, the family, the village, and the neighbourhood, are of significance for the study of them as groups. The argument is that as groups they have a structure, even if, as in many neighbourhoods, the structure is not much more than the mere juxtaposition of elements. In the structure, the persons who comprise the groups have certain positions with appropriate roles, or ways of behaving, attached to them. These ways of behaving are socially recognized, and that fact will influence the behaviour of the individual persons occupying the various positions. Of course, what we think of as individual 'personality' is of importance. Every role will be played with a certain distinctive style by the individual actor, but that very distinctive style is itself determined by the social expectations to which he or she is subjected. Individual deviance from a norm is not something which occurs *in vacuo*; it is socially determined because the norm itself is a social fact.

Another difficulty presents itself. Families, villages, and neighbourhoods provide a bewildering variety of structures. Some have been fairly carefully studied, but there remains a vast field open to future research. All that can be done here is to indicate the *kind* of structural features which are important, and give a few illustrations of the work that has been done. In the account of the work done on our third type of group, an attempt has been made to cover the whole field up to date. Here it is impossible, partly, as has been said already, because there is too much material, and partly because too little research has been done into aspects of these groups which appear to the casual observer to be of importance.

The Family. We now advance upon what is usually regarded as the most important group of all: the family. In all known societies recognition is given to some special relationship between a man and one or more women, or – less often – between a group of men, often brothers as in Tibet, and one woman, whereby the offspring, real or putative, of such unions are deemed legitimate, and have a definite place in the society. There is no evidence whatever of primitive sexual communism. The arguments based on the fact that in many primitive societies the same title is used of a number of potential 'mothers' or 'fathers' or 'brothers' or 'sisters' is not cogent. Such 'classificatory kinship names' indicate similarities of conduct, much in the way in which young men often refer to all old ladies as 'Ma' or children refer to grown-up male friends of their fathers and mothers as 'Uncle'. There is no reason to suppose that they are vestiges of a kind of sexual 'free-for-all', and in any case in such societies children are perfectly clear about who is their 'real' mother or father.

We may consider the structure of the family under three heads: the kinship ties that are effective; the relation between the members of the family; the prevailing standards of discipline.

(a) Kinship Ties. In many primitive communities that have managed to develop either agricultural or pastoral techniques to such a pitch that many people can be kept together in one place or in one nomadic community, the nuclear family of father, mother, and children is almost absorbed in a network of kinship relations, such as the clan or tribe. The life-chances of children under such circumstances are almost entirely determined by their position in the kinship scheme. Each one of them is a focal point at which a system of rights and duties meet. The details vary from culture to culture; they differ in a matrilineal society from those to be found in a patrilineal society, but wherever you have kinship groupings dominating the scene, every member has claims on particular other members, and obligations towards particular other members in virtue of some real or putative blood relationship between them.

Such systems are to be found in the past history of existing civilized societies, and of the societies of the Ancient World. They linger on in Scotland, they were characteristic of upper-class Chinese society until very recent years, to some extent they are still important among the European aristocracy, and A. D. Rees[2] reports the importance of kinship among the farmers of the district he describes.

Two developments broke them up: military expeditions and the growth of private property. Under the first, the allegiance shifts to a military leader irrespective of kinship ties. With regard to the second process: as economic techniques advance, some of the leading members of kinship groups become possessed of land and grow rich, while others remain poor and grow poorer, so that the egalitarianism of the kinship unit is destroyed. As techniques advance further and trade and industry make their appearance on a large scale, a more fundamental contradiction between kinship affiliation and the new economic system makes itself felt. Enterprise is individualistic and the standard of enterprise is efficiency; you cannot afford to promote your kinsman just because he is your blood-relation, you look for the 'best man for the job'. Chinese capitalism was hindered just because it tried to work two incompatible systems. That it is not absolutely impossible is shown by the development of Japanese industry, where the largest concerns were, indeed, family concerns, and since the war are gradually becoming so again after an abortive attempt to break them up, but this is a very rare, and possibly unique, case.

It is generally assumed that in our own society, and those like it, the family has been reduced to its nuclear essentials with only the most tenuous links with the kinship scheme to which by blood they belong. This appears to be so in America according to Talcott Parsons,[3] and may perhaps be due to their high degree of occupational and geographical mobility. Even if this be the case for the majority of American families, it may be unwise to assume that it is true of all of them; in any country, as we have already remarked, there are liable to be class differences in such matters. There certainly seem to be such differences in Great Britain. The aristocracy in England and Scotland are, one may suppose, more conscious of their kinship affiliations than are the middle class, but such social groups unfortunately remain uninvestigated by the social scientist.

In the case of the working class, however, we have some information. Dr Michael Young has carried out investigations into the kinship ties in areas of the East End of London and finds that 'the extended family is still very much a reality in the working class. . . . The immediate family, far from standing on its own in splendid isolation, is much more often part of a living extended family which includes within it three, and even four generations'. This may well be due to a fact discussed by Geoffrey Gorer in his nation-wide investigation into the characteristics of the British, that 'once English people have got a house they tend to stay in it'. 'This', says Mr Gorer, 'is probably one of the biggest contrasts between the living habits of the English and the Americans.'[4]

They stay where they are until forced or enticed to move into a housing estate with its cleaner air, its gardens, and its prestige, and then ties, which had hitherto been taken for granted, become painfully conscious. Dr Young, in the article quoted above, charges the 'planners' with ignoring the importance of kinship affiliation, and makes a plea for rebuilding urban areas rather than – or as well as – separating kinsmen by housing families miles away from their relations whose support is still of value.

The same solidarity of kin within a small range of kinship has been found by other investigators. Dr Sheldon[5] found that old people in Wolverhampton were frequently looked after by their relatives, and the same thing was found in a survey of old people living in two districts of Nottingham carried out by the Department of Social Science of Nottingham University.

Another curiosity that has emerged from research into family life is that there is a slight tendency for women when they are married to set up house near their relatives, rather than near the relatives of their husbands. Mr Mays, writing of Liverpool Dockland, tells us that: 'Where the daughter marries she often elects to live within easy calling distance of her own home, and a mile can be thought of as a wide separation'.[6] Gorer found that 'there is a marked tendency towards *matrilocality*' (a technical term for this phenomenon) 'in the English working class'. The same warm relationship between mother and daughter has been found by Dr Young in his investigation into family life in East London.[7]

One type of family life has certainly gone, and that is the extended family living under one roof. The type-case of this was the *Zadruga* of Yugoslavia. Here large kinship groups of father and mother, their sons and daughters-in-law and their grandchildren lived in a large house, or group of houses in the same compound, farming the family land on a collective basis. Such big family groups were also characteristic of the landowning classes in pre-revolution China, and also in pre-revolutionary Russia.[8]

This, of course, is one way of solving the problems of preserving family land intact, and providing a labour-force large enough to farm it. It also solves the problem of old age and dominance. Under such a system the head of the house retains his position until he dies; his sons marry and bring their wives into the household. In parts of rural Wales this is not so. The head of the house remains the head, but the sons do not marry unless they can find a separate holding of their own, and in any case the youngest son has to stay at home, unmarried, until he succeeds, while if the mother is a widow the eldest son may stay at home and may never marry at all. The average age for marriage is therefore high (31·3 years), and there are very few three-generation households.[9] This contrasts with the custom in West Ireland where the old parents move into a special part of the house when the son who will inherit takes a wife; he then becomes the head of the house.[10]

This aspect of the family – the number of persons living in it or near it, with whom a child comes into constant contact – is no mere historical curiosity. It is mentioned here by way of contrast with the small-scale households which characterize modern Western culture. If the psycho-analytic theory that we acquire our 'conscience' or 'super-ego' from our relations with adults be true – where else, indeed, could we get it from? – and if its quality is determined by the intimate emotional relations between the child and the adults upon whom it depends, then surely the number of adults upon whom it depends will make a difference. In our society a child is normally dependent entirely on the goodwill of two persons, or perhaps one person – its mother. In other societies there is a much more diffuse dependence. If it is on bad terms with one adult it can go to another for comfort.[11] On the other hand, it may result in the child having to please an audience of adults, and therefore guide its behaviour in terms of what public opinion says rather than on the dictates of a private mentor, which is encouraged to defy public opinion if it believes it to be 'wrong'. The influence of public opinion as a determinant of 'right' conduct will be mentioned later in this chapter in another context.

(b) *Relations between the members of the family.* We are here confronted with the great citadel of psycho-analysis, and if we enter it we shall never get out. We must take a firm line. According to the doctrine of psycho-analysis, using this expression to include orthodox Freudian theory, the 'neo-Freudianism' of Karen Horney, the teachings of Jung, and the Adlerian line, the development of personality can only be understood if one traces the particular emotional relationships, the pressures and strains, to which it has been subjected from infancy. The hypotheses put forward by the various 'schools' differ, but they have this in common: a child is born, it needs protection and support, this is afforded by adults, sometimes one, sometimes two, and sometimes more. They will provide the love it needs or frustrate it or both. What happens in infancy will determine its attitude, its substitute satisfactions, and, perhaps, its breakdown in future years. All this is a matter for the psychology of individual personality. What interests the social psychologist is not so much the effect of particular family relationships on the individual, as changing standards of relationship. The argument is that if, for example, you have a standard of patriarchal dominance, the pressure on all children will be such and such, though each particular instance will have its own peculiar quality, while if patriarchal dominance has been replaced by egalitarian companionship between man and wife, then the pressure on the child will be different. We are concerned here with such changing patterns, and not with the particular effects on individual personalities.

Having thus by-passed psycho-analysis, we find ourselves in something of a desert. It is by no means easy to find out about the 'formal' relationships in families on a large enough scale for generalizations to be made, even over a narrow field.

Obviously there are class differences. From casual observation one gathers that husbands and wives in the upper class live lives which are more independent the one of the other than is the case with the members of the middle classes. Some few of them may still be protected from the demands of their children by the rustling figure of a Nannie.

As usual, most of our information is about working-class families. One feature of them is also found in middle-class families as well, and that is that marriage is based on romance rather than on arrangements made, sometimes through an intermediary, independent of the wishes of the boy and girl who are to be married. This latter arrangement implies the acceptance of certain formal duties, and may well prove successful if both parties know and accept their roles. The moment mutual attraction takes the place of such established role-playing, a different set of expectations comes to the fore. More is expected of each partner in terms of intellectual and temperamental compatibility, and there is greater likelihood of disappointment. Slater and Woodside in their study of working-class marriage found 'evidence of an unrealistic and romantic attitude towards marriage. . . . Most of the subjects had married when very young, while still emotionally immature. Marriage was over-valued, and expectations were set too high'.[12, 13]

And when they are married, what is the relation between them? Of course it differs from one family to another, and doubtless under the most extreme form of patriarchalism one will find plenty of women 'wearing the trousers'. In British working-class Society there is plenty of evidence of father-dominance. 'The home', says Mr Mays of his Liverpool families, 'is in certain important respects male-dominated. The husband and father *qua* wage earner is the economic master who decides how much of the income will go to housekeeping and how much he will keep for his own personal use'.[14] He is the most important person, the final authority, but his power in the family depends partly on the extent to which he is at home. Mays quotes an article by Tom Hopkinson about family life in Bermondsey: 'Mum or Gran is queen of the family, but Dad is still king of the purse.' The importance of work is brought out in a report on Manchester dock workers. Before dock labour was regularized, the husband was 'in and out of his house at all hours of the day ... (so that) the children saw a lot of their father'. 'The close association between home and work which thus became characteristic of the dockside community has meant that the dock worker has developed a great interest in and high regard for family life'. Now, however, with more regular work, 'They are ... no longer able to keep in close touch with what is happening at home ... and find it more difficult to maintain their traditional authority in the family'.[15]

The effective dominance of the husband, then, need not correspond with his official pattern. The predominance of women in the United States of America is put down to the fact that father is out all day.[16] This will clearly have an effect, as Spinley has suggested,[17] on the 'identifications' made by the children. Her study of working-class families in a slum area in London reveals a 'family constellation of a dominant female figure ... with the corollary of a weak and probably variable male figure', and she believes that this may be responsible for 'an evident homosexual trend in adolescents, and, more significantly, adults', which displays itself in a preference for male companionship and gang life.

Reference has been made to the father as exercising control through the purse. The study of family budgeting can, indeed, be used as a method of studying family relationships. Many researches into poverty have shown that the wife seldom knows how much her husband earns, and that his contribution to her housekeeping does not rise appreciably with increase in the number of children. In Glasgow for example during the war Professor Madge found that husbands earning up to 70s. started their wives with 78 per cent of their income, rising to 84 per cent, 86 per cent, and 87 per cent with the first, second, and third child; after that there was no increase in their contribution. Those earning 100s. and more started with 42 per cent and rose to 65 per cent, 68 per cent, and 69 per cent and then, if they had more than three children, to 72 per cent. This doling out of housekeeping money, however, is not universal by any means. In Blackburn, for instance, 49 per cent gave all their earnings to their wives and received what was considered appropriate spending money. In Slough only 5 per cent of the husbands were so reckless.[18] Another study by Professor Madge and Marion Bennathan[19] is concerned with the keeping of budgets over a period of about a year. They were interested in decision-making in families, and in the sorts of topics about which decisions had to be made. Mrs Bennathan studied a small number of families intensively and it became clear that if the families were willing to co-operate much could be learnt about the relations between husband and wife by using the budget as a point of entry. Madge and Bennathan found, as one might suppose, that their families differed when subjected to detailed investigation, and one family is of special interest. Here the resources were pooled because the husband and wife shared common interests. A stress on this may, indeed, startle the middle-class reader. Surely husbands and wives share mutual interests? Not so. Casual observation, by no means a reliable guide to be sure, leads one to think that until recently it was rare for working-class husbands and wives to share any interests at all beyond the actual having of a house and, to a certain extent, the children. They are often strangers to one another. One has the impression, however, that this is changing. Education, facilities for travel, high wages, and the spread of middle-class aspirations may well lead to a change in family relationship, a change from relatively autonomous areas of interest to increased mutuality.

This approach to family relationships through their budgetary arrangements is of methodological interest. It may be remarked in passing that such researches are of immense value for the administration of the Welfare State and for the student of absenteeism. Poverty, for instance, is not merely a function of net wages; it is concerned with the amount the 'old woman' gets from her 'old man'. Under full employment, readiness to work full time, let alone readiness to work overtime, is a function of spending behaviour. This, however, is not our concern. We are interested in budgetary inquiries as a method of detecting different, and, perhaps, changing relationships between husband and wife.

Another method, far more elaborate, has been employed in Oeser and Hammond's study of *Social Structure and Personality in a City*.[20] This deals with family life in Melbourne, Australia, and we are only interested in it from a methodological point of view. P. G. Herbst, who is mainly responsible for the conceptual framework, has been influenced by the 'field theory' approach associated with the work of Lewin and his disciples (cf. p. 46).

Family life can be divided into a variety of 'regions': the wife's household duties, child care, social activities, economic activities and so on. Looking at it from this point of view you can trace the spheres of participation of the husband, the wife, and the children. Family life involves action and decision. In certain activities, the husband may decide and the wife act, or *vice versa*, both may decide and both may act, or each may decide on his or her own actions. Taking the whole range of activities into consideration one can assess the degree to which a family is autocratic, co-operative, or 'autonomic', in which case each party reserves considerable areas for private decisions. Next one can discover where tension lies, where, that is to say, disputes arise. There is highest tension where you have a husband-autocratic family, and lowest where there is co-operation. Where they tend to make their own decisions independently there is low tension in certain areas but high tension in the family as a whole. The tension reduction principle is now applied: as tension mounts 'there will be a force acting so as to bring about a state of minimum tension'. Since the maximum tension is in husband-dominated families, 'this (principle) enables one to predict with a good deal of certainty that whatever immediate changes may take place in the structure of the Australian families studied, they will be in the direction of decreasing the power field of the husband'.[21]

This is but a fragmentary account of the method of investigation, and the data to which it was applied – mainly the reports of children about their homes – are not wholly satisfactory. At the same time the Melbourne investigation is an interesting example of the application of 'field theory' concepts to the study of real-life situations.

The nuclear family consists of father and mother and their children. What about the relations between the children? Sibling jealousy is, of course, a familiar theme, and a good deal of research has been done on the influence of family position. Recently some curious facts have come to light. A study of the family positions of a group of coalminers who had been part-time students at a Midland University[22] revealed that those who were eldests were more successful in individual activities, while those who were intermediates were more successful, in after life, in group activities. The eldests had their position to maintain; the intermediates looked for support. Another investigation[23] into the relation between family position and delinquency, carried out on two samples of 206 and 502 delinquents, showed that eldests were more inclined to indulge in individual serious crimes, while the intermediates were more likely to drift into crimes as members of a gang. The youngests and only children are also individualists, and it is they who tend to come from broken homes. They are more dependent on the care of their mothers than are children in the other two positions.

(c) *Methods of Discipline*. The relation between parents and children brings us to the third aspect of the family to which we have called attention: the question of discipline. We have already said that if the establishment of a system of control depends on the relations a child has with adults, then differences in such relationships, if one compares one section of the community with another, will result in 'conscience' of a different quality. This is the theme of B. M. Spinley in the research to which we have already referred. She compared the method of upbringing employed by parents in a slum area with that employed by parents of public school boys and girls. The former were far less consistent than the latter, particular in the matter of toilet training, upon which the Freudian psycho-analysts lay much stress as a factor involved in the development of the super-ego. The slum child grows up to accept aggression as a method of getting what one wants, to demand immediate satisfaction and to resent authority. The public school boys, with their stable homes and firm discipline, acquire a strict super-ego, an acceptance of authority, and a capacity to plan for the future. This difference between methods of training and resultant class difference is not at all unlike what was found by Davis and Havighurst[24] in a similar investigation carried out in America.

In an investigation into contrasting social 'climates' in a Midland town[25] it was found that the difference in attitude to children was not merely a class matter. All the families investigated were working-class, but some were 'status aspiring' and had accepted middle-class standards, while others were 'status accepting' and had not. One can distinguish two very broad patterns. There are parents who are concerned about their children, who take their social education seriously, and hope that they will improve their position in life. There are others who, fond though they may be of their children, do not think of their upbringing as presenting a serious problem. They indulge them, and often say that they want them to have a better time than they themselves had when they were children. They do not want them to get into trouble, but, after all, children are born to get into mischief: sometimes it means the 'cops' and sometimes not. They are, in fact, easy-going. There are, of course, 'problem families' who rear their children in filth and squalor; there are, too, families who rear their children to a life of crime. Such cases are comparatively rare, though doubtless not as rare as could be wished. The indulgent, good-natured, freely expressive families, who contrast so vividly with their stricter and more conscientious neighbours, are not squalid, nor are they criminal, but they rear their children in a somewhat more negligent fashion. The controls they impart are not so strong when it comes to what we think of as social obligations. Fear of unpleasant consequences is their main concern, and this is liable to associate wrongdoing with an exciting atmosphere of risk, rather than with a sense of sin.

The significance of these differences in methods of bringing up children, differences which do not merely distinguish between one family and another, but which distinguish one sub-culture from another, for the study of delinquency scarcely needs stressing. Clearly the attitude to crime is quite different in the two types of society.

Another factor which is important in this connexion is the extent to which boys and girls regard their homes as places in which to spend whatever free time they have, or as places where you eat and sleep, refuges maybe, but not places in which to linger. 'Over the age of twelve', says Mays of his Liverpool subjects, 'boys do not spend much time in the home, except when they are sick',[26] and he goes on to say that: 'Male solidarity is a conspicuous feature of social life'. In Spinley's London slum 'The adolescent gang is an important part of social life in the area'. If a boy is not with his gang he feels ill at ease. 'Members of the gang have a strong in-group feeling; they have their own jokes, their own pubs, clubs, billiard saloons, their own intelligence service, and in-group fighting does not occur'.[27] In Bethnal Green, according to Dr Robb, children are first indulged and then, when they are likely to be a nuisance in the house, sent out to play with other children in the same plight. 'As the boy grows older the chief change in his way of life is his gradual transfer after he begins school from the group of children of mixed age and sexes to a uni-sexual gang of boys of his own age. This gang becomes one of the most important influences in his life'.[28]

The importance of the gang as representing 'the spontaneous effort of boys to create a society for themselves where none adequate exists' was studied by F. N. Thrasher, whose words we have just quoted, and whose book on *The Gang*[29] is a pioneer study of the subject. The study of gangs is extremely difficult. One has to gain their confidence, and be accepted by them as W. F. Whyte was by the *Street Corner Society*[30] which he describes so vividly in his book of that name. M. L. Turner and J. C. Spencer in an article on *Spontaneous Youth Groups and Gangs*[31] suggest that 'in the slum neighbourhood it is the gang attitudes which are the main formative influence in the ideas of adolescents'. Indeed, one might go further and suggest that wherever there is an adolescent 'peer-culture' it will have an influence which competes with that of the home. Membership involves competition for prestige, a readiness to accept the norms of the group, and a readiness to enter without fear into its adventures.

The adventures may be perfectly respectable: prodigious bicycle rides, fishing expeditions, camping, or informal football. They may, on the other hand, have a less desirable, but perfectly intelligible, sense of 'fun': breaking windows, 'scrumping', 'lorry-skipping', pilfering, breaking and entering, and so on, activities which develop into a tradition in the neighbourhood, as Mays describes in his study of Liverpool boys.

Sometimes they take to violence. This particular type of activity is socially disturbing, of course, but it raises interesting psychological questions, so far unsolved. Why violence? Professor Cohen, an American criminologist, has a theory.[32] He believes that it may be the reaction to a sense of frustration. The adolescent in our society is in an ambiguous position: neither man nor boy, and the working-class adolescent resents, in addition, his low social status. However that may be, we shall not know anything about the matter until we manage to penetrate the natural reserve of the tough gang member.

This may seem to be a digression from our main topic: methods of discipline in the family. The point is that where it is not the accepted thing for families to contain their children within their sphere of influence, they will find social satisfaction among others of the same age and in the same plight. The gang is their refuge, and its standards must be preserved at all costs.

The negative relationship between the type of family life which keeps close watch on its children and adolescents and the presence of a 'youth culture' is to be found wherever the family is a dominant institution. In an agricultural society for example in which the family farm is the main feature, boys and adolescents are introduced to agricultural occupations at an early age, and stay embedded in family life. In Cumberland, for instance, where there are scattered family farms, we are told that 'the youths of "Gosforth" are markedly apathetic and even hostile to "clubs"'.[33] There are doubtless groups of village lads who go about together, but there is no 'youth culture'.

We get an interesting sidelight on this from Dr Eisenstadt, under whose guidance a considerable amount of social research is carried on in Israel. Among the traditional Oriental families, in which occupation is tied to family life, there is a complete absence of 'youth culture'. In the co-operative settlements (Moshav and Moshava), where the family is still the unit of production, but where there is a certain amount of non-agricultural specialization, there is a certain amount of independent youth activity. In the cities, where there is still more discontinuity between family life and occupation, there is still more, while youth organizations reach their peak in the Kibbutzim, or communal farms, where family life is at a minimum and children live a great part of their lives away from their parents. The 'pioneer' atmosphere in Israel is such that most youth groups, formal and informal, are idealistic, save among the poorer classes, when they tend to be deviant.[34]

It is of interest to note in passing that in Africa, where many societies are divided into age groups, this kind of grouping is most prominent in cultures in which the kinship systems are of secondary importance.[35]

It is fairly obvious that in 'familistic' agricultural communities, there is no call for a special 'youth culture' to cater for the unattached, because the youths are never, in fact, detached from their homes. It would seem, however, that in our own society, with all its discontinuities between family life and occupation, there are sections of the community in which family unity is preserved to such an extent that a 'youth culture' scarcely develops.

We have spoken of 'tradition', 'the accepted thing', 'standards', and 'norms'. These are in part handed on from family to family in the environment in which they live. We must now turn to larger 'small groups', made up of families: the village and the neighbourhood.

CHAPTER 5

PERMANENT SMALL GROUPS

II: *The Village*

IN this chapter and the next the words 'village' and 'neighbourhood' are used to refer to rural and urban life respectively. The 'village' will therefore include what we ordinarily think of as a village and also parishes of scattered farms such as one may find in the fen district of Lincolnshire, in the north and north-west of England, and in Wales. The choice of the word 'neighbourhood' to refer to the urban environment with which a family has direct contact has been made with an eye to the literature of Town Planning. This restriction of the word to the town may be objected to. Do we not speak of a rural neighbourhood? Indeed we do, and it is almost a technical word in American rural sociology. The excuse simply is that no more convenient word for the urban context was available.

The Village. Apart from a few admirable studies, many of them unfortunately unpublished, English rural sociology can scarcely be said to exist. In what follows more questions will be asked than answered, and speculation will have to pave the way for the scientific research which will follow, let us hope, in due course.

In America a variety of economic crises and other rural problems led Theodore Roosevelt to appoint a Commission on Country Life in 1907. In 1917 the American Sociological Society established a rural section. Later on funds were forthcoming for research from the Agricultural Experiment Station and from organizations set up under the New Deal so that Professor Sims in the latest edition of his *Elements of Rural Sociology* (1940) is able to report that 'rural sociological analysis is better financed and is being more vigorously pushed than is any other branch of sociology'.[1]

This development was due not only to the need to solve the problems which were besetting the farming population, but also as an aid to the administration, which was bringing all kinds of services and amenities into the vast areas of the Middle West and West, and also into the ethnically complex areas of the South. For this reason the bulk of the research is concerned with such thinly populated areas. If, it was argued, these services were to be introduced into a scattered population, it was important to understand the social set-up.

Broadly speaking there are, in America, three main kinds of rural structure. There is the New England village, which was established in the seventeenth century by groups of immigrants, with its home lots, its strips in the arable fields allotted to different families, its co-operative methods of cultivation, and its village meeting which controlled the agricultural routine and the morals of the inhabitants.[2] In the South the colonists were richer men and brought with them the concept of the manor, which developed into the plantation. When Westward migration started, a few compact communities were established by groups of people who wished to put into operation some religious or philosophical scheme of community life, but in the main the migrants preferred a kind of lonely isolation. They did, however, keep contact with their neighbours in the interests of security, to help one another, and for social intercourse. 'Groups of neighbours', we are told, 'participated in husking, logging, house-raising, threshing, and many other types of "bees" and "socials".'[3] Dotted about were villages which provided various services for the district, and larger towns gradually made their appearance. The pioneers of rural sociology in these districts were hard put to it to discover what the rural unit was. There were townships and villages to be sure, but what other sociological units were there? They had to ask: 'By what name is the country neighbourhood called in which you live?' They took the line that people who give the same name to an area in which they live would, by that fact, show that they felt some sense of unity as co-inhabitants.

These areas, marked out by the use of a name, the American sociologists call 'neighbourhoods' – regions in which neighbouring occurs. They found, however, that the solidarity of the 'neighbourhood' is on the decline. 'As a closely-knit homogeneous group the neighbourhood is disappearing, particularly in the older, more settled areas. Informal methods of organization, while still very much a part of rural life, are being increasingly supplemented by formal organizations.'[4] In these formal relationships 'the individual, not the family, becomes the major participant'.[5]

The school is one basis of unity, the church another, the various farming organizations provide a basis of associated unity for their members, leisure-time institutions cater for the young, and the tentacles of State and Federal social and advisory services stretch out into the countryside, each impinging on particular individuals according to their particular needs and interests. Greater mobility enables people to get to the towns and villages more easily and thus the old 'neighbourhood' of neighbouring farmers is partly replaced by the 'rurban' area.

Networks of friends and kin are still, nevertheless, important. The importance of cliques is particularly stressed by Charles P. Loomis, a pioneer in the use of sociometric methods of analysis in this field. In his view: 'throughout the world, in village and isolated farming areas alike, locality groupings are not as important in personality formation and individual orientation as the smaller friendship groups.' His *Studies of Rural Social Organization*[6] contains the results of a number of sociometric analyses based on the criterion: With whom do you visit? The practical value of this is that it reveals the tendrils of the grape-vine. It is argued that if an administration or agent wants to influence a group, he must know its clique structure. In particular he must know who is an actual or potential leader, since it would be foolish to spend his time convincing someone who had no social contact whatever with anyone else.

Two other items of interest emerge from Loomis' work. By way of trying to trace the beginnings of a clique system he investigated a colony of some 600 families, settled by the Federal Emergency Relief Administration, shortly after they arrived and then after they had been there for two years. In the early days the cliques were formed on a proximity basis, but as time went on mutual interests and personal likings led to an entirely different pattern, and 'next-door-ness' was no longer so important. This finding is relevant, as we shall see, to the problem of urban neighbourhoods.

The second study of interest is concerned with another resettlement scheme in which three groups of colonists were dumped down together, two of whom were violently hostile to one another. Happily they all had a row with the government, and a sociometric analysis after that showed clearly enough that the initial hostilities had been overcome.

When we face up to the English 'village', using the word in the wide sense already mentioned, we are, of course, faced with a bewildering variety, as indeed we were when dealing with the family. In a sense the matter is worse, because every village has behind it hundreds of years of history. Just as every family has its own character, so has every village. The detailed social structure can be fully understood only if one has a grasp of the history that lies behind it. We must, however, make some crude distinctions, and if their very crudity prompts anyone to say: 'But *my* village does not fit in anywhere', so much, in a sense, the better. It will prompt the reader to ask: Why? What other distinctions ought to have been made?

To begin with we must distinguish between the compact village, whether of the 'street' type or the 'square' type with the village green in the middle, and the parish consisting of scattered farms, where the 'village', such as it is, is more like the American service station which we have just been considering, or like the villages of Westphalia which consist of little more than a church, a school, a few shops, and a post office.

Secondly, there is the distinction between farming areas in which there are large farms employing a number of farm labourers, and districts in which the farms are small family affairs with very little hired labour. In the former case there is a rural proletariat and a kind of farmer middle-class; in the latter there is much more egalitarianism. The quality of social structure is quite different in these two situations.

Thirdly, we have to remember that not all villages are agricultural. There are mining villages, villages mainly dependent on small-scale manufacture and the provision of services, tourist villages, fishing villages, and villages in which there are a considerable number of 'retired' members of the upper-middle class. What Homans calls the 'external system' – what they are there for – is different in all these cases, and therefore the 'internal systems' will be different.

In most of them one of the main features of the 'internal system', which dictates the standards of behaviour of the inhabitants, is the class structure. This is only *one* of the factors; another is occupation. The hazards of mining and the traditional occupational loyalty of the miner to his occupation (even though he often advises his sons against it) and to his mates, are different from the hazards of the fisherman and the kind of life he has to lead. In some such cases the occupational role, rather than class position, may be the most important moulding agency.

In the agricultural community, however, class distinctions nearly always play their part, except, perhaps when the community is made up entirely of smallholders, or when, as in the Welsh district described by Rees, the farming families are linked by strong kinship ties, and when even a poor man may acquire prestige through being a good singer or an effective leader in prayer.[7]

The 'ideal type' of village structure is broadly speaking something like this. At the top there is the squire or the aristocratic inhabitant of the 'great house', if there is one. Then there comes a miscellaneous group of gentry, often retired, and sometimes relatives of landed families in the county. Among the gentry we must include the parson. Then come the large farmers, and below them the school-teacher, the farm bailiff, if any, the shopkeepers, and certain skilled craftsmen. Finally there are smallholders, and, below them, the farm-workers who have their own occupational prestige scale according to their jobs: shepherd, tractor-driver, cow-man, and so on.

Such is, perhaps, the romantic notion of the village. And now we must consider some of the changes which have been going on during the last fifty years.

The 'great house' and its noble family was no doubt an object of pride and a source of bounty. Deference was demanded from tenants and cottagers, whose livelihood was partly dependent on the goodwill of its owner. Many of the working-class worked on the estate or in the house, and this dependence inculcated attitudes of respectful respectability.

All this, as we know, is a thing of the past, save in a few corners of the countryside.

The aristocrat and his family were often aloof from local affairs; they tended to consort with their kind and to fill their houses with their friends. The squire is a rather different character. He sits on the bench, on the local councils, and plays a greater part in the lives of the people about him. He too, however, is on the way out, but not so fast as his aristocratic neighbour.

The parson is still there, but he often has to look after several parishes. His position has changed, partly, perhaps, because of the inadequacies of the Church in the seventeenth century, partly because of the compensating rise of Nonconformity, and certainly because of the decline in religious practice as an accepted mark of respectability. He can no longer rely on his status as a rector or vicar; he can no longer keep up much of an appearance in the enormous rectory in which he crouches, helping his wife with the housework. He is examined as a person and criticized as a person. He has to rely on personal charm and tact as never before.

The position of shopkeeper has changed, not in prestige but in location. The butcher, the baker, the grocer all have vans, and in many villages the number of shops has declined. They get their goods delivered from the local town or from another village where a butcher or a baker has managed to survive competition. The blacksmith, too, has gone, except when he has been able to adapt his business to keep pace with mechanization.

The schoolmistress is no longer the influential figure she was. She used to teach her pupils until they left school and in many villages the youths pulled themselves together when they saw her approaching. Now, her children are whisked off in a bus when they are eleven years old. They may get a better education, but they are removed from the controlling influence of her eagle eye.

The farmer's position is somewhat ambiguous. If he comes from an upper-class family and has taken up farming, or if he has made money, he counts among the gentry. If, on the other hand, he still does a certain amount of work on the farm himself, he is in a class apart.

The greatest change has occurred among the farm-workers. This is no place to describe the history of the farm labourer. Much has been written on the subject, and a vivid account of the vicissitudes through which he has passed will be found in Victor Bonham-Carter's *The English Village*.[8] The most important changes in his life have been brought about by education, improved transport, higher wages, and fixed hours. Not so long ago he was poorly paid, badly housed, and expected to identify himself with the needs of the farm on which he worked, and on which, in some parts of the country, he lived. In the latter case, he was treated as a member of the household and expected to work without calculating his hours. The hours of work in agriculture are determined by Nature, not by machinery, though machines may shorten the time it takes to plough a field. But machines or no machines, cows have to be milked, sheep are no clock-watchers in the lambing season, and a fine light evening cannot be missed when the harvest has to be got in. The farmer, farming his own land, is tied by its demands, and naturally expected his employees to feel the same. Many of them doubtless did, and some still do, but the 'factory' spirit has reached the farm-worker, and he counts up his hours and calculates his overtime like any other worker. He recognizes himself as an employee, and in many districts this has led to a new class-consciousness. Dr Littlejohn, in one of the few sociological studies of the countryside that we have produced, tells us that in the lonely district of Eskdalemuir in the Lowlands of Scotland, the class alignment has changed in the way we have suggested. The independence of the farm-worker has led to a marked class division between him and the farmers, which has taken the place of a social structure dominated by the nobility.[9]

The long history of domination by the upper classes has left its mark on the modern village. In the old days everything was run by the gentry. They were responsible for local administration. The wife and daughters of the big house dispensed blankets and soup, and organized the flower show. In fact, with the help of the miscellaneous group of gentry living in the neighbourhood, they ran the village. They still go on in their well-cut tweeds and serviceable shoes, but running a village costs money and time, and both of these are short. They accept leadership because of their sense of responsibility and often because it is expected of them. The working-class women help them in a minor capacity, but they tend to refuse the Presidency of the Women's Institute partly because they are not used to that kind of position, partly because they are embarrassed by the upper classes, but mainly because they are afraid of the criticism of members of their own class, who would murmur to one another: 'Who does she think she is, putting herself forward?'

This heterogeneous collection of people make up the village, and the village is a face-to-face primary group. Of such groups we speak in terms of their solidarity, their vitality, and their unity. We do not expect harmony; we know that villages are rent in twain by factions: Church and Chapel, may be, or squabbles over the village hall or the siting of the sewage plant. But such quarrels may be taken as evidence of vitality; quarrels are inter-active, and when they occur about public matters the bridling, the stiffening of the back, the pursed lips and averted eyes register concern about what is best for the village.[10]

The signs of vitality and unity are difficult to determine. We look for expressions of loyalty, full houses at local events, talk about village matters, and a lively interest on the part of everyone in the affairs of everyone else.

What, we may ask, promotes such unity? We can think of four factors: isolation, work, kinship, and what may be called 'formal organization'.

(a) *Isolation.* Not so long ago, villages were isolated from one another, even though they might be geographically close. One may suppose that this would mean a firmer sense of belonging and greater social intercourse within the village, both enhanced by hostility to their neighbours. In Norfolk within living memory no young man would venture into a neighbouring village unaccompanied. In Sussex any stranger was a foreigner – 'let's 'eave a 'alf brick at 'im'. In Wales Rees reports that potential courting rivals from other villages are likely to be man-handled.[11] With the development of road and rail systems, the invention of the bicycle, the car, and the motor bus all this has changed. The villager is now familiar with the local town, the county town, and the villages nearby where he goes for whist drives, dances, and alternative brands of ale. Not only is his range increased, he is also invaded. The village is caught up in the network of social services, national trade unionism, national farmers' organizations, and the economic spirit of the time. The number of men required on farms has diminished, factories and aerodromes are accessible for work, and in many places bus-loads set off every morning to work elsewhere.

The impact of this multifarious outside world on the village has been made the subject of study by Duncan Mitchell.[12] He describes three villages, and contrasts the way modern developments have affected them. One of them, on a main road, has accommodated itself. There is a small factory; there are hotels and petrol stations; it is no longer an agricultural village, it has changed its nature. The other two, off the beaten track, have declined in population, and, so we are led to understand, in vitality. In one of them, where large-scale farming is typical, a number of villagers go off every day to work in a nearby town. There they – especially the women – acquire urban tastes, an uneasy sense of their not being quite up to them, and a competitive spirit which drives them to display increasing signs of sophistication. The children at 11 + go off to the town for their schooling and misbehave when they get back. All this has led to a decline in village activities. The third village, composed of smallholders or small-scale farmers, has resisted all change. They are suspicious of education, as something imposed from outside, they are alleged to have refused a bus service, they are deficient in such amenities as water and electricity, in fact they have tried to resist all interference, and social activity is at a low ebb.

In another comparative study, this time of ten villages, Mitchell[13] has suggested a fourfold classification of types of response to the invasion of the countryside by urban influences. There is firstly the 'closed, but integrated' community, which has resisted change and yet has preserved its vitality. Such may be found in out-of-the-way places, protected by geographical remoteness. Secondly there is the type of village which obstinately remains 'closed' but from which life has departed; strangers are suspect, the young tend to leave, and those who remain have not the heart to develop activities on their own. Thirdly we have the 'open, but not integrated' type. The new dissolving agencies are there all right, but they merely dissolve. The buses carry the villagers off elsewhere for their amusements, social life in the village is at a low ebb, not because the inhabitants have no heart, but because their hearts are elsewhere. Finally there is the health- ier alternative to the first response – the 'open and integrated' type, in which the village has become transformed from its old pattern, but has retained its vitality in a new shape. New associ- ational bonds are forged which bring the villagers into touch with outside organizations, individuals pursue their individual interests in company with others like-minded; the original close- knitness is replaced by a more flexible network of associations, but the village as such still retains its identity in more than a purely geographical sense. Such, it will be suggested, is the shape of the village of the future.

In the remoter regions of Wales, Eskdalemuir, and Cumber- land, the change in attitude to work has been noted; it is due to the absorption of these areas into the national system of institu- tions. Furthermore, the farms are no longer run on a subsistence basis; commercialization, with its individualistic accompani- ments, has changed the attitude of farmers to their neighbours, who are now their rivals. In such scattered districts, too, another minor change has appeared. A great deal of social life was medi- ated by travelling pedlars, postmen, milkmen, and so on. They had time to stop for a gossip, and, if they came on foot, were glad to sit awhile by the fireside. Now, Rees complains, there is no time; they come in machines and want to get away as quickly as possible.

All this means an increase and a widening of individual attach- ments. Individuals find their interests catered for farther afield, the various national Services impinge on each in a way slightly different from the way they impinge on his neighbours, a higher standard of leisure-time activities is demanded, and the village boundary is no longer the horizon of its inhabitants.

(b) *Work*. Just as the fact of living in the same place induces a certain sense of unity, so does the fact of earning one's living in the same way. In a purely agricultural village, where very few go away to work, the common occupation of the villagers gives them something of a fellow-feeling towards one another, and enables them to know one another better.

Working conditions in the past, however, have involved more co-operation than is the case at the present time. In the Middle Ages, for instance, up to about 1350, and in many areas after that date, farming over a large part of England was carried on in the open fields, of which there were two, three, or four, and in which individual holdings were marked out in strips. After the harvest cattle and sheep were turned out in the field which had been harvested, and there were common rights over meadow and woodland. We need not go into the vexed question of communal ownership as being characteristic of early settlements, the open-field system certainly involved communal decisions, as it still does in Laxton (Nottinghamshire) where the open-field system is still working.

Such co-operation, which must have had a unifying influence in the past in England, in the rest of Europe, including the Russian Mir, and in the New England settlements of America, is now a thing of the past. In the more scattered districts, however, a somewhat different form of co-operation has survived until recent years. Where there are scattered family subsistence farms the work was done by the family and such few farm-hands as were employed. There are, however, recurrent crises in farming life, when more hands are needed, and there is always an *ad hoc* need for tools that your neighbour has and you have not. Thus in Cumberland we are told that reciprocal aid was expected between one farm and another, irrespective of the persons actually occupying the farms. In Wales local custom determines with which of his neighbours a farmer co-operates, and when a farm changes hands the newcomer takes over the obligations of the farm; lending implements and helping with the harvest were bound to the land, like the suit to the Sheriff's Court in the Middle Ages. In Eskdalemuir there used to be a general party to help with the shearing which went from farm to farm. This has now declined. Farmers prefer to be independent, and like the farmers of Westphalia, they do not like their neighbours to see too much, nor do they like to be 'beholden'.

Commercial farming and mechanization have combined to reduce the amount of mutual aid to a minimum, and the necessity for co-operation has ceased to be a unifying force.

(c) *Kinship*. We have already noted that a network of kin links the farming community described by Rees; it is also reported from Cumberland, but on the whole it seems to play but little part in the rest of England. In many villages to be sure there are complicated ramifications of kin, but further research would be required to find out how important it is as a unifying force in village life.

(d) '*Formal organization*'. In the Middle Ages the affairs of the village were controlled by its reeve, and by the Court Baron and Court Leet of the manor which were responsible, broadly speaking, for civil and criminal issues respectively. To these Courts certain of the inhabitants owed suit, and these participated in the running of their affairs. Bit by bit, after the decline of feudalism, the Church took over, and in 1601 'the Poor Law formally placed all responsibility for village affairs upon the shoulders of the Vestry'.[14] In particular the Vestry had responsibility for the poor under the various arrangements that were made up to 1834 when the administration of the Poor Law was transferred to the guardians of 'Unions' of parishes under the control of the Poor Law Commissioners in London.

In the Middle Ages, too, there was another scheme of formal control: the 'frankpledge' system. Most of the able-bodied men were grouped in 'tithings' of ten, or sometimes twelve, each responsible for the good behaviour of the others, and headed by a 'tithing-man' whose duty it was to report the misdeeds of his tithing to the appropriate quarters. The scheme was not universal, and sometimes whole villages would form a 'tithing', but where it existed it was the duty of the Sheriff or some other person who had the 'view of frankpledge' to see that everyone who ought to be in a tithing was so enrolled. This method of keeping order was employed quite recently in pre-revolutionary China by the

Kuomingtang in 1932, in the institution known as Pao Chia in which ten households were formed into a 'Chia' and ten chia into a 'Pao'. The purpose was, by enforcing mutual responsibility, to detect the subtle influence of Communism.

These ancient institutions of control must have meant that many people were involved in the village as an administrative unit, and thus have identified themselves the more with it. The modern parish council dates from 1894, and its vitality varies from one village to another. It has few powers, but it has the right, and indeed the duty, to initiate action on the part of other bodies. On the whole one suspects that its vitality depends very largely on crises: the need for more houses made more insistent by the horrid spectacle of houses being built in the next parish, and the need for water, electricity, and other amenities. It is argued that if it had greater powers, it would be more active in focusing the interest of the villagers on their common problems.

From all this it would appear that the factors which in the past have no doubt heightened the amount of interaction in the village have ceased to be important. Villages are no longer isolated, co-operation is not what it was, and the powers of the Parish Council are insignificant compared with the power of the Church exercised through the Vestry.

In his account of the 'disintegration' of 'Hilltown', a rather remote farming community in New England, Homans[15] describes how up to about 1900 the farms were largely self-supporting, how they helped one another, and how the 'town' meeting acted as a kind of 'court of first instance'. The norms of morality were strict, and the power of the religious communities was strong. And then commercialism crept in, industry came near, and all was changed. The organization that had existed ceased to exist, and the high standard of morality declined.

Homans then proceeds to enunciate several hypotheses. 'A decrease in the frequency of interaction', he said, 'will bring about a decrease in the strength of inter-personal sentiments', and 'a decline in the extent to which norms are common and clear.' There is no longer that watchfulness of the behaviour of others which close interaction breeds.

It is rather absurd to compare a democratic New England

village with its 'town' meeting, with the non-democratic British village dominated for so long by the Church and the Gentry. We know too little about the norms of behaviour in villages in the past. And yet future research, using Homans's concepts, might reveal interesting principles of change. So far as informal agencies of control go, they have certainly lost ground.

Speaking at a meeting in 1846, James Silk Buckingham remarked that 'if a man lived in a village . . . where all his movements were seen and known, he would be a much better man . . . and if a man did wrong under such circumstances no one would speak to him; he would find the place insupportable and would be compelled to go away'.[16] Who would say that now? In Wales the 'seiat', at which the public confessed their sins in full Chapel, is a thing of the past. Oddly enough one gets the impression that the lads of the village were often the guardians of sexual morality. In Wales, Rees tells us that men who misbehave with women may be seized and covered with dung. In Sussex they played 'rough music' on a variety of kitchen implements under the windows of the sinful. In Germany they strewed chaff on the road between the houses of pairs suspected of having extra-marital relations. They are too much engaged with other things to do that now.

We read of the 'disintegration' of the village, and in two of the villages described by Duncan Mitchell the word is not, perhaps, inappropriate. But how can one tell when social life has 'disintegrated', and not merely changed into something else? Where, as in these two villages, the population has declined, one can point to the fact that they have shrunk; once there were a lot of shops, now there are none, and so on. This, however, is by no means common. Perhaps the best test, which has already been suggested, is the existence of well-attended societies. In a survey of a rural area of Germany,[17] on which industrialism has encroached, the authors remark that sports clubs and glee clubs serve as an integrative force because the members come from all walks of life. Is this not happening in British villages?

We have assumed that in the past the fact that they lived together in an isolated spot, the fact that they were all occupied in the same way, the fact that they were under the domination of the same persons, the big farmer, the parson, and the squire, and the fact that these last took responsibility for village affairs, somehow welded them all into some kind of whole. We imagine that they all had some fellow feeling, combined with appropriate attitudes of deference and patronage, for one another, and a general loyalty to the village as their home.

Much of this has changed with the changing years, save perhaps the loyalty and affection for the place of their birth. But with the changing years has come leisure and new interests. It is in the development of sectional organizations, each catering for special interests of all the inhabitants, irrespective of status, that we may see, not the disintegration of social life, but its enhancement. There are local football and cricket leagues in which village plays village, there are village dramatic societies which compete with one another at drama festivals; groups of villagers can hire a bus for an expedition, and above all there are the Women's Institutes to which all classes belong and at which the most retiring can be 'brought out' by competitions, little exhibitions, and simple games. These are but a handful of village activities. Where they flourish we can say that the village is alive.

CHAPTER 6

PERMANENT SMALL GROUPS

III: The Neighbourhood

THE village is is often held up to us as a model. 'The English village', writes Thomas Sharp, 'is, I believe, among the pleasantest and most warmly human places that men have ever built to live in.' In the previous chapter some attempt has been made to display the complexity of the village social structure, and the changes which it has undergone. It is often thought of as providing the type example of a close-knit community in which everyone has his place and his respected status, a place in which the individual is secure and not overwhelmed by the vast anonymous mass of the great conurbations.

In the city, we are told: 'Man is submerged in the colossal human swarm, his individuality overwhelmed, his personality negated, his essential dignity is lost in crowds without a sense of community.'[1] Lewis Mumford cries out for: 'Small groups: small classes: small communities: institutions framed to the human scale.'[2]

These assertions about the sense of community in the village, and the 'negation' of the personality in the towns, are based upon no solid foundations whatever. The village is practically always seen through the eyes of the middle class and there is very little evidence of the deleterious effect of city life. In the village you are likely to know your neighbours, in the town you often do not. This is considered a sad state of affairs. Why? What we do know is that many city dwellers who were evacuated into the country were so horrified by the silence and sparseness of the population that they quickly made tracks for home. The countryman, when he goes to the big city, is bewildered by the noise and the crowds, but there is no reason to suppose that the townsman longs for the peace of the countryside.

However, out of a great deal of nostalgic romanticism, some good has come. Surveys have been made of town life, particularly of slum life, and careful studies have been made of life on housing estates which have often been planned so as to provide that neighbourliness in which the city is alleged to be so deficient. There is, thus, a considerable amount of material which it is impossible to summarize in a short space. Only some of the more important considerations will be discussed.

The word 'neighbourhood' presents difficulties. Any town can be divided into relatively homogeneous areas. There is the centre, there are residential areas, there are working-class areas. These last two are sometimes segregated from the rest of the environment by main roads, railways, by some distinctive feature of the landscape, as when a park has been turned into a residential area, or by the fact that they are inhabited by a distinct ethnic group. These are sometimes called 'neighbourhoods'. The unity of such areas is sometimes recognized by the people who live in them, and the aggregate is thus made more of a 'psychological' neighbourhood, in which the inhabitants do most of their shopping and spend a good deal of their leisure time. The public houses are 'locals', have their 'regulars', and are quite different in quality from the public house in the centre of the city.

Such physical neighbourhoods, however, are face-to-face groups only in a very tenuous sense. In many of them, particularly the 'residential' neighbourhoods, there is but little overt neighbouring, and, indeed, it is sometimes said that there is no neighbouring in cities at all, or only very little.

Mr Gorer in his survey of the English character found that 'The stereotype of the lack of neighbourliness in metropolises or big towns is amply confirmed', and that 'the stereotype of the women popping round next door is not borne out'.[3] This may be because the people who do pop in are not the sort of people who fill in questionnaires.

It is difficult to know how much popping in is actually part of a local pattern. In the East End of London it is common enough. Michael Young, writing of Bethnal Green, describes how long residence in one place, which often means going to the same school, makes for neighbourliness. He quotes an inhabitant: 'Around here you know everyone. I was born here and so were all the other people. If you haven't got a sister you can leave the children with, there's always someone you know from being at school together. "Look, Harry," you can say, "look after Betty for a couple of hours. I want to go to the shops."' A simple and, indeed, obvious assertion, perhaps, but this kind of thing is never mentioned by those who complain of the 'impersonal' quality of city life.

In parts of the Black Country we are told that: '"Popping in" to see neighbours was particularly common in older areas, especially in the back-to-back streets.'[4] In two streets in a Midland town which were compared in the research to which reference has already been made,[5] it was found that they had quite different standards of neighbourliness. In one they 'kept themselves to themselves', in the other they were constantly in and out of one another's houses.

Certainly reserve is not universal, and when there is considerable interaction between neighbours the street, the court, the alley, or the lane is more than a mere aggregate of dwellings. The physical neighbourhood is distinguished by its inhabitants as an entity, it is thought of with affection, and besides knowing one another socially the neighbours may indulge in collective action. The Coronation decorations in the street in the Midland town in which there was a great deal of interaction were a magnificent collective effort, only just defeated in the competition by another street of the same kind. The 'respectable' street merely produced a variegated display of shabby individual efforts.

In Liverpool we are informed by Mr Mays[6] that the boys have for a long time established a tradition of inter-street football matches. While it is true that the boys form a peer-group, as we have already said, it is likely that some sense of the street as a distinctive unit lies at the back of this choice of team-formation.

In Bethnal Green, to quote Michael Young again: 'If there is a sense of belonging to Bethnal Green, there is an even more marked sense of attachment to that bit of it in which people happen to live.' These 'bits' may be just alleys or 'turnings'. '"In our turning we do this that or the other"', they would say. '"I've lived in this turning for fifty years", said one old man proudly, "and here I intend to stay". Many of the turnings have little War Memorials to their men killed in the 1914–18 war. This kind of attachment is even stronger in the small courts where a few houses face one another across a common front yard. In one of these the houses are covered from top to bottom with green trellis work, tiers of window-boxes stand out from the trellis, and on one wall there is a proliferation of flowers around a kind of shrine which encases a Union Jack and two pictures of the Queen.'

In such small areas one does have groups which are 'face-to-face' groups in a fairly full sense. These units, however, are nothing like so clearly defined as are those which are to be found in the cities of China and Japan.

In the People's Republic of China, cities are divided into Wards, like our own, but the Wards are divided into 'neighbourhoods' made up of a group of 'alleys'. The families in the 'neighbourhood', living as they do in courtyards, elect a chairman, and representatives on the various Committees. The Committees are concerned with women's welfare, care of the dependents of the armed forces, the tidiness of the streets, literacy, and the general good behaviour of the people living in the 'neighbourhood' they represent. They vie with one another in local social activities, and one 'Alley leader' pointed with pride to the little litter baskets they had hung on the telegraph posts, a convenience which had been copied by other neighbourhood units.

It is partly through the activity of these units that Chinese cities have been freed from flies, and their inhabitants made so health-conscious that it is common to see young men bicycling through the streets wearing gauze masks over their mouths. When a judge was asked about juvenile delinquency, his reply was that the neighbourhoods see to that. When a man applying for a divorce was reprimanded for having a 'feudal' attitude towards his wife and was told that he needed 're-educating', it was made clear afterwards by the presiding judge that the re-education would be done by the 'neighbourhood'.

These units of collective action are powerful agents of social control and they act as a two-way avenue of communication up to the municipal authorities, and down from the central Government through various intervening bodies.

Such relatively small units would seem to have a spontaneous basis, which the present régime is exploiting. In Chinese villages, we are told the neighbours living in the five houses on each side of any given house form a unit for the central house, to which a special name, *Shan-lin*, is given. They have special obligations towards one another.[7]

In Japanese cities they have associations called *tonari-gumi*, made up of from ten to twenty households. The newcomer is expected to call on the members of the *tonari-gumi* he is about to join, and leave a small present at each house. The members of the households are expected to help one another when there are difficulties, to take note of weddings and births, and, in particular, to rally round when there is a funeral.[8]

In America the Chicago Area Project, started in the 1930s under the guidance of Clifford R. Shaw, has been attempting to 'aid the development of independent, indigenous groups of local residents to take the leadership and assume the responsibility in managing, financing, and promoting welfare programs in their neighbourhoods'.[9] These groups were mainly formed to provide a check to juvenile delinquency, the argument being that the neighbourhood sets the tone and that it is no use removing a delinquent from a neighbourhood whose standards are undesirable and then plunging him back again after 'treatment' in prison or at some other penal institution. 'Change the street', is the slogan.

In towns the neighbourhoods, in the sense of aggregates of homes occupied by people of roughly the same income group, have developed haphazard. In some of them there is a vague sense of unity, and in some of the working-class areas smaller groups can be found in which the sense of belonging is very much more intense. The general picture of unplanned growth is, however, distasteful; town and country should be planned. New houses are needed to replace the slums and to house the growing population. Let them be built in a more orderly fashion than has been the case in the past.

Two themes can be distinguished in the programme of the planners: the amenity theme and the community theme. The first is concerned with the convenient siting of services, such as shops, clinics, community centres and so on, and also with ensuring the safety of the children by so arranging the houses that they are not on the main road. The houses may be arranged in cul-de-sacs, and squares or courts, or in any other way which will deter the children from darting out of the house and making straight for the oncoming traffic.

To talk of 'cul-de-sacs or courts', as if it did not matter which, is, however, most improper when we come to the second theme: community. Here we are concerned not with amenity, not with safety, but with the personality which is said to be 'negated' in the city. It is never easy to discover exactly what dream is in the minds of those planners who talk so fervently about the 'sense of community', which they seem to think so desirable. They want people to be 'neighbourly'; they do not seem quite to approve of people just having a few friends in remote parts whom they like to visit, they want them to take an interest in the affairs of the locality in which they live. Perhaps they envisage a community as a kind of purée, mashed strawberries and cream, strongly flavoured with the 'we-feeling'. Perhaps they are intermediate children (see p. 69). Perhaps they are just lonely and think everybody else is. Anyway, they certainly aim at making the new towns and new housing estates into 'real communities'.

The resettlement of households on estates of various shapes and sizes has given rise to a variety of investigations by the social scientists. What, they ask, actually happens?

Let us start with America. Leon Festinger and his colleagues Stanley Schachter and Kurt Back describe the way in which social relations are influenced by the physical arrangement of the houses in which the participants live.[10] Two adjoining estates were established in 1945 to house veterans and their families who were attending the Massachusetts Institute of Technology. One project, Westgate, consisted of houses arranged in courtyards of from seven to thirteen houses each, the other, Westgate West, consisted of seventeen two-floor converted Navy barracks. Each of these latter groups of buildings contained five households with separate entrances on the ground floor, and five households on the upper floor, each entered from a balcony, which was reached by a staircase at either end. The hypothesis was that friendship would develop on a basis of 'passive contacts' made going to and from home. Sure enough the sociometric assessment, on the criterion 'What three people in Westgate or Westgate West do you see most of socially', showed that the friendship choices declined with distance. In the courts of Westgate next-door neighbours were mentioned as friends more than people farther off, and people tended to have friends in their own courts rather than in the others. In Westgate West there was a similar verification of the hypothesis: next-door neighbours were friendly and so were the people who lived at the tops and bottoms of the staircases, but on the upper floor physical distance was not so important because everyone used the common staircases. By way of proving the rule it was shown that people living in end houses, facing the street, got fewer choices as friends because their paths did not cross the paths of their neighbours so frequently.

There was a Tenants' Organization which started under difficulties, and the tenants were asked whether they approved of it or not, and whether they took part in it. It was found that on the whole *courts* agreed in their approval or disapproval, and that this agreement was the most marked in those courts with the largest number of mutual friendship choices.

'In a community of people who are homogeneous with respect to many of the factors which determine the development of friendships, the physical factors arising from the arrangement of houses are major determinants of what friendships will develop and what social groups will be formed.' Such is the conclusion of Festinger, Schachter, and Back.

The same influence of spatial location was found by Merton,[11] save that according to him there is a greater tendency to select friends directly across the street. This may possibly be influenced by whether the front of the house is much used as 'living space' or not.

Festinger's housing project was inhabited, as he says, by a homogeneous population. The housing estates to which we are about to refer are homogeneous in the sense that they would be called 'working class' but, as we shall see, they are heterogeneous with respect to status and to attitudes towards neighbouring.

Leo Kuper investigated a housing estate in the neighbourhood of Coventry. There, as in Westgate, the houses were arranged round courts. They were two-storey, semi-detached houses, with front doors facing the court, and side doors facing one another. They had gardens behind and no garden in front so that anyone could look into the houses from the court, and, indeed, the people living in one side of the court could see into the houses opposite. Just as in Westgate, 'Active sociable relationships are maintained primarily within the sub-unit', and 'within the sub-units the main area of sociable activity is the immediately proximate. Relations with neighbours on either side of the informant constitute half the total number of internal relationships.'[12] So far, the findings of Festinger seem to be confirmed, but closer inspection revealed a rift on the estate. Some people referred to their neighbours as 'scruffy' and 'ignorant', and their children as 'dragged up not brought up', while their neighbours referred to them as 'high and mighty', 'stuck up', and thinking too much of themselves. We come upon the distinction between the 'respectable' and the 'rough'.

In the light of this the two back doors which open on to one another, with their adjacent lavatories in full view, now take on a more dramatic role. In Westgate, no doubt, the emerging householders would fall into one another's arms. In Braydon Road, Coventry, on the other hand: 'This enhanced importance of proximity is, however, expressed in two entirely opposed ways: on the one hand it promotes adjustment and friendship formation, and on the other hand, tension and withdrawal.'[13] From Liverpool we hear: 'Whilst next-door neighbours may become friendly they may equally well become bitterly hostile to one another ... it does not seem possible to assert that the spatial position of the houses contributes either one way or the other to the formation of friendships.'[14] From Sheffield we learn: 'It is often the juxtaposition of people with different individual attributes which produces social conflict.'[15]

The Liverpool estate was built in 1942–3 to house the families of men working in nearby factories. It was, therefore, primarily working class, with a sprinkling of foremen and clerks. Here, again, two status groups are formed, not, as one might suppose, foremen and clerks on the one hand and the rest on the other, but two status groups differentiating the bulk of the population, excluding the foremen and clerks, and irrespective of grade of occupation. The foremen and their wives take little part in the social life of the estate. This is in accord with the principles associated with formal leadership. Their leadership role in the factory is carried over into the estate, and it is difficult for both parties to adjust to a different social relationship. 'The assumption of superior status on the estates by persons who wield authority at work tends to be keenly resented, and it is probable that it is more difficult for those who have had authority conferred on them in one context to acquire it in the other.'[16]

The situation of the foremen is fairly straightforward, the status-differentiation of the bulk of the residents is less obvious. The authors of the Liverpool report make an interesting suggestion. Speaking of the tendency to 'assume social status', that is to say to adopt a reserved and, in the eyes of their neighbours, a 'stuck-up' attitude, they suggest that 'this is a social technique devised to enable them to maintain social distance and preserve the prerogative of choice in situations in which this is sometimes difficult'.[17]

The authors of the Sheffield report make a slightly different, but not incompatible, point. The estate with which they were concerned was started in 1923 as a rehousing project on which the families living in slum areas were rehoused street by street. The latest wave of immigrants thought themselves a cut above the earlier inhabitants, but from the description and the reputation of the estate one gathers that it was pretty homogeneous from the class point of view. They all moved from the 'intimacies of the slums, where behaviour is relatively uninhibited' to a new environment which provided a 'more restrictive and isolated existence'. Some, we are led to understand, were not deterred by this, others found the adjustment difficult and became reserved and careful in their new relationship with their old friends. They were, in fact, 'living up to' the new and more respectable environment.

The neighbourliness between neighbours, then, depends upon the attitude of each towards neighbourliness. The attitude towards the community as a whole, the community spirit, is bound to be influenced by this heterogeneity. One thing draws them together, and that is a crisis. The Residents' Association on the Liverpool estate was formed to deal with the local authorities, the Community Centre on the Sheffield estate was formed in 1933 to provide a club for the unemployed, and the same kind of co-operative effort has been noted elsewhere – by Ruth Durant, for example, in her study of *Watling*.[18] When the crisis is over, the collective enthusiasm tends to evaporate, and the community organization may cease to exist. If it continues to exist, because there are residents who are prepared to take steps to keep it going, it may cater for the 'respectable' and not the 'rough', or *vice versa*. Of the Liverpool estate centre we hear that its existence 'appears to accentuate divisions between the inhabitants'.

One important factor that we have already noted in village life is the presence of leaders. This is why the Liverpool estate continues to have a Community Centre, even though it is not patronized by all sections of the community. Absence of leaders is responsible for the collapse of the centre on the Sheffield estate. 'There has always been a tendency to resent any attempt on the part of ordinary workers to assume a leadership role as "uppish".'[19] The leaders, therefore, must be drawn from among persons who are accepted as of superior status, but who are not too remote from those they are to lead.

The significance of the Liverpool and Sheffield studies lies in the analysis of the background of the inhabitants of the estates. Everyone admits that the siting of houses is important. We learn from Kuper that neighbours will behave to one another in terms of their attitudes to neighbouring. We learn from the Liverpool and Sheffield studies that this attitude will be determined by the traditions which the inhabitants have brought with them, by their aspirations, and sometimes by their work-relationship (cf. the foremen on the Liverpool estate). Whether estates should be 'mixed' or not is a vexed question. Kuper seems against it;[20] the authors of the Sheffield report think that 'mixture does provide a wider range of visible ideals which can lead to changed aspirations and a different style of living'.[21] If mixing is decided on, it must be remembered that there are two kinds of neighbouring, which Dr Peter Mann[22] calls 'overt' and 'latent'. The former is the gossipy kind, the latter the reserved kind. For the latter the good neighbour is one who respects one's privacy, but because of that very fact he may be a good *neighbour*.

One suggestion, made by the joint authors of the Liverpool and Sheffield studies, which also reminds us of a point made about the vitality of village life, is that a way to enliven community life in estates may be through appealing to sectional interests. To expect people who don't mix to enjoy a general 'get-together' may indeed be hopeless, but to cater for individual interests in dancing, drama, music, sport, and child-care may bring people together who would not otherwise meet.

Tradition has been mentioned. It is no good expecting a hand-some physical lay-out to be used as it was intended, if the customs of the inhabitants are against it. Many people have what might be called a 'back-door' culture. The mothers spend most of their time in the back part of the house and the children play there. It is not unknown for people removed to housing estates, con-structed on up-to-date Raburn principles with nice grass courts for the kiddies to play in, to ignore such delightful amenities and enjoy a lively social life at the back of their houses. You can try to counter this by putting the dustbin outside the front door, but in all probability this will merely mean that the housewives will be put to inconvenience.

The siting of houses is by no means unimportant, but of greater importance are the attitudes, habits, and aspirations of the people who live in them, and this can only be discovered by research of the type we have been considering.

Planned Communities. The village and the town just grow, without – until recently – any overriding plan to control their growth, and certainly without any intention to create a social community. Housing estates are certainly planned, and, as we have seen, their sizes and shapes are intended somehow or other to promote a sense of community by the judicious placing of the houses. There is, however, a class of community in which the order of planning is almost reversed, communities in which the community spirit might be said to precede its physical habitat. In villages, urban neighbourhoods, and housing estates the inhabitants live private lives, some of them see a lot of their neighbours and enjoy it, some of them see very little of their neighbours and prefer it that way. Some of them identify themselves with the community as a whole, and try to 'get things going', while the rest sit back and have things done for them in which they participate or not as they think fit. In the type of community we are now about to consider everybody is expected to put the interests of the community first, and their own private lives last.

Again, it is impossible to cover the whole field; we can only mention a few representative examples.

The basis of these communities is a revulsion from modern capitalistic society, with its selfish profit-seeking, its concentration on material goods, and the disparity of reward which differentiates societies into the rich and poor. The positive inspiration comes from religion, political idealism, or a mixture of these and a devotion to the welfare of a nation.

Many such communities were founded in America in the early nineteenth century.[23] There were Ebeneza and Amana, the homes of 'True Inspiration Congregations' founded by Christian Metz and Barbara Heynemann, where they had periodical inquisitions of the whole community at which each member was expected to confess his sins. Any unadmitted shortcoming was detected by specially inspired persons.

At Zoar lived the Society of the Separatists, founded by Joseph Bäumcher, where marriage was considered on the whole unfavourable to the community life, but not fatally adverse.

The Shakers, followers of Ann Lee, were also celibate, and insisted that only the simple labours and manners of a farming people can hold a community together. Manufacturing spells disaster.

At Oneida and Wallingford, on the other hand, the Perfectionists went in for a kind of 'complex marriage' on the grounds that no one should be so selfish as to unite himself with one woman to the exclusion of others. They, too, had occasions for mutual criticism and public reprimand.

All these were based on religious fervour. The Icarians were a non-religious society of liberal intellectuals founded by Étienne Cabet. So too was Robert Owen's experiment founded in 1825 on land bought from the followers of George Rapp, and sadly miscalled 'New Harmony'. The members consisted of some 900 people drawn from all parts of the United States and after living together in acrimony for three years the society dissolved. When the end came, Owen said: 'This proves that families trained in the individual system have not acquired those moral characteristics of forbearance and charity necessary for confidence and harmony; for communities to be successful, they must consist of persons devoid of prejudice and possessed of moral feelings in unison with the laws of human nature.'[24]

Most of these societies have been short-lived. They had many difficulties in their way: the personal charm of the founder cannot last for ever, and there is always the problem of a successor; sex is always a disturbing force, and it is thought by some that social cohesiveness is necessarily in inverse relationship to sexual licence;[25] a fervent and deviant religious belief is hard to maintain and notoriously liable to schism; economic problems must be faced, for even a spiritual community must live, and economic difficulties and chance disasters are liable to breed despair; finally there is the outside world washing up on the shores of these islands of communism and carrying its sons and daughters away. It may be that 'national character' favours or impedes the prosperity of such groups. Nordhoff, in his survey of communistic societies in the United States, remarks: 'the Germans make better communists than any other people', adding, curiously enough in the light of subsequent events, 'unless the Chinese should some day turn their attention to communism'.[26]

They have not all perished by any manner of means, and new ones are being founded. The Huterites, whose church dates back to the teaching of Jacob Huter in the sixteenth century, numbered some 8,542 in 1950, and the Society of Brothers, who were ejected from Germany in 1937, founded a flourishing Bruderhof at Wheathill in Shropshire, others in Paraguay and in America.

The sad fate of many of these communities, their idealistic merits, and a desire to promote co-operation have inspired Henrik F. Infield[27] to examine some of the communities that survive, in order to discover wherein lie their weakness and their strength. To do this he uses a battery of tests: questionnaires to elicit degree of co-operativeness, and the source of satisfaction-dissatisfaction with the community, and a sociometric test designed to find out the degree of mutual friendship which pervades the society.

With these tools, for instance, he compared two settlements: 'Matador', a group of fifteen war veterans settled in Saskatchewan, and 'Macedonia', a group of fifteen conscientious objectors settled in Georgia. The sociometric test was devised to enable him to compare choices on the criteria of work with choices based on criteria of companionship – talking over personal problems, and sharing leisure-time pursuits. In 'Matador' the basis of choice was much more concerned with work; in 'Macedonia' it was the other way round; they seemed keener on valuing people for their friendliness than for their skill. From this he inferred that 'Matador' might find difficulty in facing disaster because there was but little solidarity except in the economic sphere, while in 'Macedonia' they were better placed, though they should pay more attention to work than they did.

This advice was, indeed, taken, and in 1952 their solidarity had improved on all fronts since the first assessment in 1947. Disaster, however, lay ahead. Disease, fire, and economic disorder put them to the test. Four important members left, dissension broke out, some of the members joined up with a Bruderhof founded by the Society of Brothers, but half of them determined to see that 'Macedonia' lived on.

Another study, this time of 'Clermont', a community of work in France, brings out the same point as was made about 'Matador'. This community, living scattered about in a town of some 30,000 inhabitants in the south-east of France, has a factory in which the 115 *productifs* work, and attached to them are the 63 *familiers* who are members by virtue of marriage to a productive companion. Out of work the whole body, together with candidates for admission and apprentices, conceive of themselves as forming a *groupe de quartier*, and this group is considered to be of paramount importance. On closer investigation with the battery of tests mentioned above it was found that the social life, which was the main point of the group, was by no means all it set out to be. It looked as though newcomers were chosen for their engineering skill rather than for their social co-operative-ness. 'It is not easy,' says Infield, 'to balance the requirements for a material basis with those for a social organization based on comprehensive co-operation.'[28]

The older societies believed that initial goodwill would be enough. Infield's researches have shown that the establishment of such communities in a world which does not share their ideals is far more complicated than one might have thought. They also show that something can be done to diagnose defects and to discover ways of dealing with them.

Enthusiasm, however, is clearly needed, and it is possible that the enthusiasm of a group may spread techniques of co-operation throughout the larger society. Perhaps this may happen in Nigeria, where some 2,000 Negroes, holding their goods in common, have settled at Aizetoro and engage in agriculture and fishing. They are known as the Holy Apostles, and live a life of pure communism, conforming to the principle 'from each according to his capacity and to each according to his need'. They seem to be successful economically, and if that is the case, they might prompt the rest of the community to try large-scale farming which would, we are led to understand, be an advantage over the present arrangements.[29]

In all these cases the society in which the communities are established is either antipathetic or indifferent to their principles. In Israel all is different. Here some form of communistic idealism is the officially recognized doctrine. Israel is the Land of Promise, the land in which poverty and misery are to be abolished. It is a land of pioneers in new ways of living. Of course, as Dr Eisenstadt has shown, this 'pioneering spirit' is by no means universal. Successive waves of immigration have brought people with a variety of traditions, skills, and hopes. Their assimilation is fraught with difficulties, but communistic communities do not have to fight for their existence, they are publicly encouraged.

The settlements are by no means all communistic. There are purely individualistic settlements (Moshavot) and co-operative villages (Moshavim and Moshav Ordim) in which there are family holdings and distribution of profits to every family, according to their contribution. As with the Russian Mir there are sometimes re-distributions of land according to changing labour forces in households.

The Kvutza and the Kibbutz, however, are purely communistic with payment according to needs. There is the very minimum of family life, children being brought up in separate establishments and visiting their parents from time to time. In all these settlements the principle of 'self-labour' is accepted; there must be no exploitation of others; all must work for the community and thus for Israel.

Of course, in spite of public approval and encouragement, there are difficulties. They recognize that communal life puts a strain on everybody at first, and that mere enthusiasm, without what Owen called 'forbearance and charity' and without staying power in the face of disaster, is not enough. For those who elect to join a Kvutza or a Kibbutz they have wisely established training institutions where candidates who are likely to prove unsuitable can be weeded out.

Another difficulty springs from political theory. There are, very naturally, those who feel that the principles of Marxism are not sufficiently recognized; there are those who see no reason why they should be. However, one gathers that the Community movement in the Kvutza and the Kibbutz is a success.

As to the Russian and Chinese experiments, very little can be said. The structure of the collective farm in Russia with its family holdings, its committees, and its teams of workers in the fields, in the orchards, and in the byres is well known. The welfare of the collective as a whole is a matter of concern to everyone, because everyone shares in the profits, but the weight of the administration falls on a comparatively small number of persons, albeit elected by the members of the collectivity. How far the individual householder identifies himself with the collective is hard to say. From cartoons in *Krokodil*, representing workers busy, all too busy, on their own allotments, one gets the impression that here and there, at any rate, the communal spirit may be found wanting.

In China the collective farm movement is, we are told, proceeding rapidly. Based, as they are, on the peasantry, the régime has so far taken a very sensible line. The peasants have just got the land they have longed for; why should they welcome its being –

as they would think – taken away from them? The first thing they did was to encourage 'mutual aid teams', and this is pretty well universal. They help one another, and help those who cannot help themselves: the widows and the sick. The next step is co-operation and then collectivization which is to be established by 1960. In both countries private ownership and private sharing of profits is regarded as a 'contradiction', which will – nay, must – be resolved.

CHAPTER 7

EXPERIMENTAL GROUPS

I: Working Together

IN this and the following chapters we shall be concerned with experimental evidence with regard to the third type of group referred to in Chapter 4.[1] So much work has been done that selection and arrangement have presented difficulties. A group solving a problem, or engaged in any task, must be thought of as an integrated structure which comprises the activities required by the task situation and the emotional relations between the members. Bearing this in mind, however, we can consider their interaction from two points of view, roughly corresponding to Homans' 'external' and 'internal' systems. Since interaction affects sentiments, and vice versa, these two aspects can never be held completely apart, but in order to reduce the mass of material to some kind of order, we shall lay emphasis in this chapter on the task aspect, and in Chapter 9 on the emotional aspect. Nevertheless, it has to be admitted that a certain amount of overlap is unavoidable.

The presence of an audience. Before we discuss experiments on group interaction, we must mention some pioneer work on the influence of an audience on the performance of a person who is being watched. As early as 1903 in Wurzburg, Auguste Mayer[2] found that when subjects did mental and written arithmetic, or learned nonsense syllables, or completed sentences before an audience, there was from 30–50 per cent improvement, and, surprisingly enough there were fewer errors made. Since then numbers of subjects have been subjected to the eagle eye of observation, even, as in the case of Laird's[3] students, to a chorus of abuse. The technique is straightforward. You test the subjects out separately and then make them perform in front of a small or relatively large number of onlookers. F. H. Allport[4] found that ergograph results (the lifting of a weight with one finger) and

106

dynamometer tests improved when an audience was present. G. S. Gates,[5] on the other hand, found that an audience had no general effect on the total performances of the subjects taken together, except in word-naming, but it also turned out that the subjects who scored lowest by themselves did improve in the presence of the audience far more than was the case with such of the high scorers as improved as well. Travis[6] got his subjects to perform a hand and eye co-ordination test in which mistakes were registered by a buzzer, and he found that 18 of his 22 subjects made a better maximum performance in front of onlookers and 16 of them made their highest score under these conditions.

The most elaborate studies were made by Dashiell.[7] He used as his tests multiplication, a mixed relations test, and serial association. His subjects worked alone, under observation, merely together, and competing with one another. He compared the results of their activities except the last with respect to accuracy and speed. The results are somewhat complicated, as one might expect, but the general upshot is that observation improves speed but diminishes accuracy. Rivalry speeded up the serial association, but the effects of working together were not well-marked. F. H. Allport,[8] on the other hand, working with the 'together' situation, found that this improved free association, with the curious additional fact that when working alone the associations were more personal than was the case when working in the presence of others doing the same thing. When it came to writing out arguments, the amount that was written was greater in the 'together' situation, but the quality poorer.

Whittemore,[9] too, found the same contrast – improvement in speed and the reverse in accuracy, and the same result was found by Moede[10] in Germany. Whittemore's experiments, however, bring out something else as well. He told his subjects on some occasions to compete, on other occasions not to compete. The latter was almost impossible to achieve. Of course, when one group was pitted against another the output was greatly increased. A little more is added by Mukerji.[11] His subjects, who had to name capital cities and do cancellation tests, improved when working together, but there was great fluctuation in their speeds. This might be due to the extra spurts of effort which had to be produced in order to overcome the distraction caused by the presence of other people. This extra effort was also noted by Sengupta and Sinha,[12] who also used cancellation tests.

The knowledge of other people's scores may make a difference to the individual's prediction of his own future performance, his 'level of aspiration' as it is called. This may turn out somewhat unexpectedly. Hilgard, Sait, and Magaret[13] told a group of students their speed scores in an arithmetic test at intervals, and asked what they thought they would do in the future. The high scorers predicted a lower score, the low scorers a higher one. This is in line with some more of F. H. Allport's work. He asked his subjects to judge weights and assess the unpleasantness of smells on a scale. They did this at first privately and then in the presence of one another. In the latter situation the judgements were not nearly so extreme as they were in the former. 'The fact of shunning extremes and expressing more moderate estimates when in the presence of other judges, seems well established.'[14] This so-called 'levelling' process can also be seen in the frequently reported cases of the greatest improvement being found among the slowest workers.

In 'real-life' situations something of the same kind has been observed. Wyatt, Frost, and Stock[15] found that workers sitting next to one another or opposite one another varied together in their output. Whitehead[16] has shown that the girls who worked on relay assembly in the Hawthorn Works, sitting round a table, tended to work at the same speed as their friends. Lorenz,[17] working in Germany, reports that women sitting six at a table carrying out one process of making a gym shoe were more efficient than when working separately, but that if you put a good group between two poor ones it goes down, while the reverse happens if you put a poor one between two good ones.

It is now time to attempt a summary of all these findings. In the first place it is clear that working in the presence of others, whether acting as an audience or doing the same kind of thing, makes a difference to the performance of the individual. In many cases there is an improvement. F. H. Allport explains this with the expression: 'social facilitation', which tells us precisely nothing; it is merely an alternative way of stating the facts to be explained. The clue perhaps lies in the contrast between quantity which increases and quality which is impaired. As Dr Klein[18] points out, speed and quantity of output are obvious to the lookers-on; accuracy and intellectual skills are not. The individual in our society is out to shine; he therefore automatically goes for that characteristic of his work which everybody can judge. This, doubtless, accounts for the improvement in Travis's subjects. They were going to demonstrate their skill in the hand and eye co-ordination test and everyone could see how good they were; the buzzer announced their failure to the world.

This is not to deny the influence of embarrassment, which has also been noted. No doubt an extra effort has to be put forward to combat it, and this effort may show itself in output; no doubt, too, embarrassment affects intellectual operations more than mechanical ones. The factors at work are complex, but the almost universal finding of improvement in quantity does seem to suggest that this is at any rate partially due to its public nature.

The influence of the group, taken as a whole, is seen in the 'levelling' process. No one wants to be too different from or too far below the average. Extremes are avoided because the individual does not want to be, in Allport's words 'at odds with the judgement' (and, we would add, 'performance') of his associates. At the same time he does not want to fall below the others, so that if he is slow he will put on an extra spurt; the good and the average can rest on their oars. Another factor may well be the security that is felt in finding agreement, especially in a situation in which there is no obvious right answer.

This last point is illustrated by a celebrated experiment carried out by Sherif.[19] He exploited an odd phenomenon of perception. If you go into a completely dark room and a small light is seen, so dim that it does not illuminate the walls of the room, it will appear to move. Subjects who are asked to estimate the amount of movement, not knowing that it is not really moving at all, make various guesses and then settle down to a uniform assessment. When several subjects are invited to judge the apparent distance moved together, any of them speaking first, they start by giving their own assessment, acquired when making judgements by themselves; after a while their assessments become more and more alike, converging to a mean. In an ambiguous situation we seek a firm frame of reference. If the outlines of the room are visible, they form a frame of reference in which, of course, the light is seen to be stationary; in the dark we are lost and have to supply our own. With other people we may be said to seek support from them.

Are two heads better than one? The experiments with which we have so far been concerned are not experiments in group interaction; they are concerned with the influence of the presence of other people on individual performance. We must now turn to experiments in the co-operative solution of problems. Before dealing with these, however, we should note two sets of experiments which deal with the question at the head of this section in a different way. Supposing a number of people make judgements, which are then averaged by a central authority, in these cases the experimenter, will the pooled judgements give a better answer to the problem than individual ones? Knight[20] was a pioneer in this kind of inquiry in 1921. She invited individual estimates of the I.Q. of children judged from photographs, of the effectiveness of fifteen advertisements, and of the temperature of the room. The individual judgements differed widely in their accuracy, so did the pooled judgements when the three types of estimate are compared. In the first task the pooled judgements correlated $+\cdot26$ with the objective standard, in the second $+\cdot63$, and in the third the average estimate was pretty close to the temperature of the room: 72·4 to actual 72. In all cases there were some individuals better than the group; in all of them most individuals were worse than the group. Knight was followed by Gordon,[21] only one of whose experiments need concern us. She had 200 subjects, who were asked to rank weights which were very like one another in descending order of heaviness. Here again the range of individual variations was very large, correlating with the objective order from $+\cdot95$ to $-\cdot81$. She then took at random 40 groups of 5, 20 groups of 10, and 5 groups of 50, calculated the 'group judgement' for each group, and the mean of group judgements. For groups of 5 the mean judgement for all of them correlated with the objective score $+\cdot68$; the composite score for groups of 10 correlated at $+\cdot79$, while the individual group scores for the groups of 50 correlated at $+\cdot92$, $+\cdot92$, $+\cdot94$, and $+\cdot95$, the latter being the same as the best individual score. It looks as though for simple tasks, involving what we should regard as a purely objective measure, a pooled judgement may be as good as the best individual one, provided enough judgements are pooled; where what we think of as 'subjective' factors enter, as is the case with the estimates of intelligence from photographs or the efficacy of advertisements, there are likely to be experts about whose judgement is more accurate than that of a group.

These two experiments do not involve any discussion. When discussion enters in the results will depend on the grouping of the subjects, as Jenness[22] found when she got her subjects to estimate the number of beans in a jar. They made their estimates separately at first and then, in groups of 3 or 4, they voiced their judgements and discussed them. When the groups were made up of members who differed, and became aware of the difference of opinion, the final estimates became more accurate – they converged, in fact. When, on the other hand, the groups were made up of members whose opinions were alike, whether in over-estimation or under-estimation, their discussion did not improve matters; in fact they supported one another in error.

In the last experiment, discussion has made its appearance. We must now consider some of the enormous mass of material explicitly concerned with that subject. Broadly speaking it is concerned with two aspects, the first arising out of the question: 'Are two heads better than one?' with the attendant question: 'How many cooks spoil the broth?' in the background, the second and more recent preoccupation being with the actual process of discussion and inter-communication itself. In this section we shall be concerned with the former of these two topics, in the next with the latter.

One of the most important studies in this field was made by Shaw[23] in 1930. The pattern of the experiments is already familiar: individual work compared with group work. Her material consisted of those well-known teasers which present, for example, the predicament of missionaries and cannibals crossing a river in a boat which only holds two at the same time, ensuring that the cannibals on either side must never outnumber the missionaries. It was found that only 5 correct solutions out of a possible 63 were discovered by individuals, while 8 correct solutions out of a possible 15 were discovered by the groups. From an analysis of the number of suggestions made and corrected, it looks as though this superiority of groups over individuals is due to the presence of people with bright ideas, and also of critics. The initiator of suggestions did not reject his own suggestion as often as other people, which indeed is not surprising, but the presence of critics was clearly of the utmost importance.

The same results had already been indicated by Watson[24] a year or so earlier. He used a number of different types of problem, and the group result was better than the average individual performance every time, but some of his tasks displayed group superiority more clearly than others. They were better at finding words meaning the opposite of given words, and also at solving ciphers, whereas they were not so much better than the best individuals at reading comprehension, the comparison of numbers, and composing limericks. This brings out the value of more heads than one. Each suggestion of a word by a member scored in the opposites test, and criticisms as well as suggestions were valuable in the other one.

Thorndike[25] strikes a new note. With no less than 1,200 students working in groups of 4, 5, and 6, selecting the better of two poems, the more favourable of two attitudes, and judging the truth or falsity of factual assertions, he found that after discussion the percentage of problems for which the 'correct' solution is found rises. He put this down to the fact that individual subjects tended to agree with the majority and that the majority were persuaded by the confidence of the members who knew the 'correct' answer. Stress is also laid on the confidence of the expert by Gurnee.[26] He first used an entirely different type of experiment. His subjects had to find the correct path in a maze by using a stylus, and it was so arranged that a light indicated whether the right path was found or not. Individuals did it separately and groups tackled it, using the technique of majority decision at turning points. They did this six times, and after the first one the groups improved more than the individuals working alone did.

However, on the seventh trial each member of the groups had a go by himself, and each was no better than the individuals who had worked alone. Was the group success due to some kind of averaging out of individual errors? In a second experiment, using verbal tests and, again, majority voting, Gurnee came to the conclusion that the superiority of the groups was not to be explained on statistical grounds, but was really due to the fact that the subjects who were right were quick to voice their views and that the others followed them. The confident expert has made his appearance.

The topics chosen by Thorndike raise an important problem. Judging the better of two poems and giving the answers to geographical, historical, and other problems are two very different types of activity. In the second case there are accepted criteria of right answers; in the first this is not so. A technique often adopted is to accept the judgement of a panel of experts, as was done by Timmons,[27] who set his subjects to discuss ways of improving the parole system in the State of Ohio, and found that group discussion produced results judged by experts to be better than those suggested by individuals, and that this could not be explained in terms of the pooling of the suggestions of the members of the group. We may accept the expert judgement as a device for producing an objective standard, but clearly this distinction between material that is a matter of opinion, and material that involves a clear right and wrong answer, obvious to anyone when it is pointed out, is a matter of significance with respect to the part played by members of discussion groups.

Thorndike,[28] himself, appreciated the importance of the type of task and experimented with a large variety of problems, much as Watson had done. He included vocabulary tests, completion of limericks, and the solution and construction of crossword puzzles. He presented his tests in two forms, free and constricted: the vocabulary test could be completed freely or by choosing from alternatives provided; the limericks had to have either three more lines, or only one more; and it was argued that the construction of a crossword puzzle was 'freer' than finding a solution to one already made up. The groups did better on all tests than individuals, but, as was expected, their superiority was more marked in the 'free' form of the first two tests than in the restricted form. When it came to the crossword puzzles, however, this was reversed. In the first two, bright ideas are valuable and can be used by the other members of the group, either as adding something in their own right or as putting other ideas into the minds of the rest of the party. In the construction of a crossword puzzle on the other hand a plethora of suggestions may do more harm than good, because it involves elaborate planning in which a keyword dictates the other words required for the rest of the puzzle. Here an individual might get on better by himself. Solving a crossword puzzle is a very different story; here division of labour is possible.

This came out in a mechanical experiment carried out by McCreedy and Lambert.[29] There were six switches so wired to a control panel that a certain arrangement of them made a light go on. Individual workers manipulated all the switches, groups of 3 operated two each. Individuals were better at it than groups. McCreedy and Lambert put this down to inattention, arguing that in the discussion which the groups were permitted to engage in, it was very likely that one of the members would not pay attention, and would mess up the plan of the others. Scoring was calculated in terms of the number of solutions in a given time, and the very fact of discussing may have influenced the group scores, apart from inattention. One cannot, however, resist the suggestion that groups could not plan their campaign as well as individuals.

The possibility of the division of labour as an important factor making for group superiority was brought out by Husband,[30] who compared people working by themselves with people working in pairs, solving word puzzles, jig-saw puzzles, and arithmetical problems. Pairs were better than individuals in the first two tests because division of labour was possible.

All this is pretty familiar in everyday life. When co-ordinated planning is needed the individual working alone may be more efficient than a group; where division of labour is possible, or where you want a number of new ideas, or criticism on the part of people who may not be particularly productive themselves, two heads may be better than one. When the results of the individual's lucubrations have to be translated into action by people who have played no part in the decision-making process, the *total* efficiency may on occasion be reduced, but that is another story.

We must now consider some of the evidence concerning appropriate sizes of groups. In 1927, South[31] compared groups of 3 and groups of 6, working on matching photographs with the names of emotions, rating pieces of prose composition, bridge problems, and multiple choice problems, involving rational learning. It will be noticed that the first two, which South tiresomely called 'concrete' problems, are largely matters of opinion, the second two, which he equally tiresomely called 'abstract', are such that a solution is pretty clear when found. Neither sized group did better at the bridge problems than the other, but small groups were better at guessing the emotions registered in the photographs, and assessing the merit of the pieces of prose, while the larger groups were better at the reasoning problems.

The principles which are at work here are fairly clear. When matters of opinion are at stake individuals very often have strong ones, as South discovered in his 'concrete' problems. It therefore takes some time for an agreed decision to be reached, and *that*, in such test situations, is the solution of the problem. Obviously a small number of people will be quicker at coming to some kind of agreement than a large number. Deutsch,[32] for instance, found that when he compared discussion on problems of human relations with discussion on the solution of a logical puzzle, there was more interaction and attention to what was being said when the groups were talking about the former than when they were talking about the latter. This must mean that solution, which here is agreement, is delayed in the 'opinion' situation.

On the other hand, when you have a problem with a solution, the more participants you have the better, with some reservation to be mentioned below. A large group is more likely to contain the expert who sees the solution, or helps towards it; it is more likely to contain helpful critics, and more likely to have people in it whose suggestions are valuable in bringing up new material to set the others thinking again. In 1924, for instance, Bechterev and Lange[33] working in Russia got audiences to look at pictures and then report details they had observed or similarities between pairs, or impressions made. They then discussed among themselves and made another attempt. The discussion had added details, and points of view, and the second set of reports were either fuller than the first or altered by the new points of view that had been voiced. Whether the members will contribute with additional information, suggested solutions, criticism, or new points of view will, of course, depend upon the problem.

Size, however, brings its own peculiarities. South compared groups of 3 with groups of 6. Gibb[34] went further than that. He compared groups of different sizes up to a membership of 96. They discussed a problem for half an hour and then the members called out their solutions and they were put up on a blackboard. He found that the productivity of a group varies negatively with the size of the group, and that, as groups get larger, individual members tend to feel more inhibited. The particular form the experiment took was certainly calculated to produce embarrassment in the more shy participants, and, as Kelley and Thibaut[35] observe, a problem may have only a few different solutions, so that when the more vocal members have uttered these there is little call for productivity on the part of the rest. However, the inhibiting influence of large numbers is an important factor.

Carter[36] found that this change of climate, as one might call it, varies with quite small numbers. His groups of 4 were freer to express their ideas than were the members of groups of 8, when only the forceful members dominated the scene. Bales, Strodtbeck, Mills, and Roseborough[37] found that the proportion of infrequent contribution increases as the size of the group increases, while Stephan and Mishler[38] show the other side of the picture, namely that as size increases, even within the range of 3 to 7 the amount contributed by the most active members increases as compared with the amount contributed by the rest. In fact, at a relatively low level of size, leadership displays itself.

Of course, the influence of size on the individual member will vary with his motives, his loquacity, and the subject-matter of the discussion. However, in addition to these personal differences and difference of topic, it does look as though a more general principle were at work, reducing an increasing number of people to silence as the size of the group increases. This is, no doubt, extremely gratifying, but unhappily it is not always the right people who are silenced. We have already indicated that where matters of fact are involved the more potential contributors and critics the better, so that the weight of the group may act like an ox sitting on the wrong tongues. The bore, alas, is seldom unnerved; that, indeed, is why he is a bore.

All that has so far been reported brings out into the open matters of common experience. We apply the principles thus revealed in many cases. We recognize that certain problems of policy can best be discussed by a small committee, we invite individuals to work out solutions of problems when division of labour is impossible, and we co-opt people on to committees if they have specialist knowledge. Other things, however, have to be taken into consideration. We are frequently forced to have large committees because all 'interests' have to be represented, and because people like to feel 'in on' decision making, even if they do not participate vocally.

Much, of course, can be done to ensure that the members of even small committees make what contribution they can. This was put to the test by Maier and Solem.[39] They compared small groups of 5 or 6 whose chosen chairman merely acted as an observer, with similar groups whose chairman was instructed to act as a leader, encouraging the others to express their opinions. The latter groups were more successful at solving problems than the former, though they were matched for ability before the experiment began. This was because the 'leader' tried to ensure that all the latent talent in his group should be made use of.

Competition. So far we have been concerned with groups co-operating with one another. What happens when a group is constituted of members competing with one another? Mintz[40] demonstrates one result. He used a kind of parlour game. Each of his subjects was supplied with a string attached to a cone in a bottle. Some of his groups were told that individual rewards and fines would be given to those who extracted their cones; the other groups were told that it was an exercise in co-operation. Not surprisingly there were endless traffic jams in the first type of group, while the others proceeded with elegant co-ordination. Of course, the trouble was that the competitors seeking rewards and avoiding being fined got in each other's way. A group of people competing *separately*, so that their actions do not interfere with one another, may be more efficient in total output than if competition was ruled out.

In discussion groups the element of competition is likely to produce a complete change of atmosphere. Deutsch[41] divided the members of a psychology class into two types of group, telling one of them that the group score obtained by solving problems in human relations would count towards their grading in the course, and the other that individual contributions would count towards the grading of the individuals who made them. The results bring out the virtues of co-operation. The co-operating groups produced more, the members had a greater sense of responsibility, produced more diverse contributions, were more attentive to one another, more friendly, and enjoyed themselves more. The competitive ones were obviously anxious to restrict communication in the interests of personal victory, and less interested in what the others said because they were intent on their own success.

Two types of task were used, logical problems and problems in human relations. In the former the co-operative group interacted more than the competitive group because the solution of logical problems did not positively require discussion; the competitives did not want to give anything away, the co-operators wanted every idea to be put forward in the interests of the group. The human relations task, which had no solution in the sense that the logical one had, produced opposite results. The competitors wanted to pick each other's brains, to criticize each other's suggestions, and to make their own contribution triumph.

An incidental difference worth noticing was that there was more 'substitutability' among the co-operators than among the competitors. If two or more people are aiming at the same goal so that the actions of each are helpful to the actions of all, they will readily accept a step forward on the part of one member as a 'substitute' for that step in their own progress; if the success of one is injurious to the success of the others, this will not be so. This is a direct deduction from the general principles of field theory.

The advantages of co-operation are, it may be argued, just what we should expect; the characteristics we think of as 'team spirit' are present. We might, however, ask ourselves whether educationalists make enough use of the principles enunciated in formidable detail by Deutsch. Do we, perhaps, use individual competition too much? In the People's Republic of China they make conscious use of co-operation. In the gardens of the University of Peking on a hot August afternoon, a group of students were sitting in a circle. Why were they there when the rest of the students were away on their holidays? Because one of the party had been ill and had fallen behind with her work; the others were coaching her because it would be a disgrace if any member of the class failed in the examination. Some English children who had been educated in a Chinese post-revolutionary school and came to England found the atmosphere of competition quite bewildering.

In everyday life situations the factors which the experimentalists try to disentangle are mixed up. They usually are concerned, for example, both with matters of opinion mixed up with matters of fact. They are ostensibly co-operative, but we all know that the spirit of competition is by no means always absent; that is why they often last so long. Fouriezos, Hull, and Guetzkow[42] took the trouble to watch no less than seventy-two actual conferences and noted the extent to which the members were activated by self-centred motives, wanting to gain points, to attract attention, to get something off their chests, and so on. The more of these there were at any meeting the less likely they were to get through their agendas, and when asked afterwards the members expressed greater dissatisfaction with such results as they had reached. So far as the observers themselves were concerned we may note the sustaining power of the scientific spirit.

Another study, very much more detailed, of discussion groups in several sessions, working under laboratory conditions, was carried out by Heinicke and Bales.[43] They found that in their four one-hour sessions there was persistent disagreement during the second session. Four of the groups got over this for the other two sessions, while the other six did not. Cross-questioned afterwards, the members of the four groups who settled down agreed among themselves as to who were the leaders; they agreed on a status order. The other six groups had no such agreement among their members. Heinicke and Bales suggest that this is due to a kind of jockeying for position, a struggle for status. How often have we experienced that! When status is settled co-operation can begin in earnest.

Although we have mentioned experimental work done in recent years, the general topic of the effectiveness of groups has on the whole given way to an interest in the actual behaviour within the groups themselves, how they communicate with one another, the stresses and strains that occur, and the pattern of interaction that unfolds itself. To such investigations we turn in the next chapter.

CHAPTER 8

EXPERIMENTAL GROUPS

II: Communication and Patterns of Interaction

THE problem of communication is one that exercises many minds. It almost has publicity value; it is certain to be mentioned in any discussion on the principles of management, so much so that one writer[1] on industrial topics has asked whether 'communication' has acquired the status of a 'sacred cow'. Whether people are being mesmerized into thinking that all industrial problems can be solved by improving communications or not, the subject is clearly of importance. Whether you are concerned with the institution of government or industry, with the organization of the Services or of the Church, nothing can possibly be done in a co-ordinated way without communication. Someone has to say something to someone else, face to face or through an instrument, or else he has to write something to someone else and communicate an order for transmission. We think of government services, industrial units, and trade unions as organisms which ought, if all is well, to work like clockwork. In fact, of course, they consist of a network of communications, verbal or written, and the larger they get the more paper they use.

The system may be faulty in various ways, of which the most important are: speed, completeness, direction, rigidity, and phraseology.

When a system of communication expands, it may take longer for messages to pass from one end to another. Technical devices, such as loud speakers, may overcome this, but they cannot always do so. This is particularly the case where the system is divided into a central executive office and branches which are geographically separated from it. It takes time to inform the central office of the problems of the branches, it takes time for them to reach a decision, and when they have done so, and the decision is communicated, the situation at the periphery may have changed. This leads to exasperation at both ends. It is this time-lag that undoubtedly plays a part – not the only part, to be sure – in the discords which occur in the field of trade unionism; branches have complaints, the central office takes a long time dealing with them, and unofficial strike action is frequently the result.

By incompleteness in a communication system is meant the absence of links in the chain, which means that everybody who ought to be informed is not in fact informed. This may be due to a variety of causes. It may be that it is not the job of anyone to inform a particular person or group of persons. This is fairly easy to set right by working out a chart of communications; if it is not it leads not only to gross inefficiency at some point in the system, but also to friction and a sense of frustration on the part of those who are left out of the scheme, and have to get their information through informal channels or by chance. Faulty linkage may, of course, be due to the withholding of information on personal grounds of dislike or irritation. Again it may be due to a well-meaning attempt to ensure communication between the extremes, resulting in by-passing the people in between. It has been pointed out that this is liable to occur when joint consultation is introduced; the foremen may be the last to hear of decisions that have been made, and hear it, when they do, from the shop-floor. Not unnaturally this makes them rather cross. Finally a network may be incomplete through the sheer absence, through illness or some other cause, of a member in the chain. Where there are several sub-systems linked together by single individuals, obviously these persons occupy key positions in the network. If they fail to communicate because they are not there to do so, the situation is far worse than if one of the peripheral members were absent.

A system of communication is defective in direction if only one direction is made possible. Systems are usually devised to ensure that communication passes from high status to lower, down the line. This is required for the passage downward of commands which those at the bottom of the scale have to carry out. For a command to be effective, however, the person who issues it must be in a position to assume: (a) that it will be carried out; and (b) that it is appropriate. If there is no upward movement of communication this assumption cannot always be made. In addition to this, unless there is a two-way system of communication complaints and frustrations will pile up at the bottom and ultimately impair efficiency.

The problem set by the need for speed, completeness, and a two-way system of communication might be solved by careful thought and clear, diagrammatic planning. There is, however, a danger lurking here: the danger of rigidity. A system must be flexible enough to operate in a crisis. Such flexibility may, of course, be ensured by informal communication, by goodwill, and by initiative, but any hierarchical system of communication in which each level can only communicate with the one immediately above or below, while it has obvious advantages, may become so ingrained in those who operate it that it breaks down under stress. It is obvious that the larger the number of interconnecting positions in the scheme, the less this is likely to occur.

Finally, under 'phraseology' we must refer to a different aspect of communication altogether. It would seem to be a point scarcely worth mentioning to say that a communication should be such that it is understood by the person or persons to whom it is made. The facts are not as simple as they might appear at first sight. We need not bother about the problem of a foreign language which has to be translated, though commands are frequently issued in a language 'foreign', in some sense of the word, to those who receive them. Even granted that the actual words are understood, they may be, and all too often are, interpreted in a sense quite other than that intended by the speaker. What is said is received by the hearer in a frame of reference which gives them their meaning to him. This includes not only those mechanisms whereby we literally understand the spoken word, but also a set of attitudes, expectations, fears, and suspicions which enable us to understand, as we fondly think, what the other person is 'really getting at'. His tone of voice, his gestures, and his general demeanour are all relevant.

This is well brought out in the report of the Acton Society[2] entitled the 'Workers' Point of View', which is concerned with the problem of joint consultation in the mining industry. It is no earthly use for managements in any industry to view arguments for joint consultation and for 'putting the workers in the picture' with complacency, if the workers interpret their efforts as merely an advanced method of throwing dust in their eyes. To complain that they are misunderstood merely shows that they themselves are lacking in understanding. When the relations in industry have been embittered by what is deemed by the workers to be callous exploitation, it is extremely difficult for the communications from above not to be misinterpreted by those to whom they are addressed, but efficiency of communication depends on the avoidance of such misunderstanding.

In some situations, even in the absence of suspicion and hostility, there may be systematic divergences of interest which make communication between two parties difficult. Divergence of interest between employee and employer is a case in point, but there may be divergence of interest even when ostensibly the interests of the parties are alike. The central executive bodies of the great trade unions are not only far away from their branches, they have interests which diverge from those whose interests they are there to further. A great national concern has national responsibilities and is also concerned with the welfare of all its members. The members of a particular branch are interested in their own problems and want them settled as soon as possible. They see their problem from their own point of view; to the central executive body it is seen in the light of a whole range of national and industrial policies, and, if the Union is a multiple industry one, they see a particular dispute in relation to the interests of the other industries with which they are concerned. This systematic divergence of interests is, of course, not confined to industry; it is present in the relations between government at all levels and the citizen. The citizen may want a house, the U.D.C. has to consider his claim in relation to all other claims, in relation to their budget and in relation to various regulations by which they have to abide. The citizen can perfectly well understand the letter of refusal, it is all too clear, but he may well interpret it as yet another instance of incompetence and corruption.

Enough has been said to show the importance of the problems presented by communications, and it is not surprising that they have become a topic for discussion and exploration.

One form of investigation is common enough: the inquiry made by industrial psychologists when something has gone wrong. With these we shall not be concerned.[3] The question before us here is: What contribution has been made by the experimental social psychologist?

Of recent years an attempt has been made to compare patterns of communications on a very small scale to see whether any principles emerge. Such an enterprise must of necessity simplify the whole problem and therefore be somewhat remote from the real-life situation. This, as has already been said, is inherent in experimental procedure.

The research to which we are going to refer is of methodological interest. The pioneer in 1948 was Alex Bavelas,[4] a follower of Kurt Lewin. The pattern of procedure of many of the Field Theorists is to work out from a few very elementary assumptions what is likely to take place under certain conditions, and then to construct an experimental situation in which their deductions can be tested. Such, it may be said, is the proper procedure in all scientific inquiry: the formulation of hypotheses and their testing. This is perfectly true, but the Field Theorists present their reports very often in a formal manner which is not very widespread among social psychologists. Attention has been called to this in order to place the work we are going to consider in its methodological setting.

Bavelas's pioneer work was followed by the experimental researches of Harold J. Leavitt,[5] and it is from his work that we take our account.

Supposing we consider the following simple designs as patterns of communication; the circles represent persons and the lines represent connecting links of communication.

A	B	C	D
Circle	*Chain*	*Y*	*Wheel*

In the 'circle' each person can communicate with two others on either side of him; in the 'chain', if A or E want to communicate with one another they have to go through three other people; in 'Y' and the 'wheel' one individual, C in both cases, occupies a key position. C also holds a key position of a rather less obvious kind in the chain. Supposing each member of the chain has a piece of information which has to be put together to solve a problem. It would be possible for A to tell B, for B to add his bit and tell C, for C to pass a message on to D, and D to E. On the other hand it would be quicker if A and B told C, and E and D told C, so that C could put all the information together with his own and then communicate with B and D, who would tell A and E respectively.

Bavelas provides us with a device for measuring this feature of 'centrality'. First add up all the steps which each person has to take to communicate in the shortest way with everyone else. Thus in the circle $AB = 1$, $AC = 2$, $AE = 1$, $AD = 2$, making 6 in all. This must be the same for all the others. Then add up all these totals, which in the circle come to 30. Now divide the total for each with the grand total and you get the 'centrality' of each. In the circle they are all equal. Consider, however, the 'Y' system. $AC = 1$, $AB = 2$, $AD = 2$, $AE = 3$, making a total of 8. B's total will be the same, but $CA = 1$, $CB = 1$, $CD = 1$, $CE = 2$, making 5 in all. $DC = 1$, $DA = 2$, $DB = 2$, $DE = 1$, making 6, and $ED = 1$, $EC = 2$, $EA = 3$, $EB = 3$, making 9. Thus we have $8+8+5+6+9 = 36$. A's score is 4·5, B's is 4·5, C's is 7·2, D's is 6·0, and E's is 4·0. C's 'centrality' score is the highest, but not so high as it is in the 'wheel'. The scores for the members in the other figures are worked out in the same way and have been written in in the diagram.

Another measure is the 'diameter', the shortest distance between members farthest apart. In the 'circle' and the 'wheel' everyone can reach everyone else in 2 steps; in the 'chain' A takes 4 steps to reach E; in the 'Y' A and B take 3 steps to reach E. The times taken for all members to be informed is a function of the diameter.

These are purely formal properties of communication systems, and can be measured for similar systems of any size. The next problem was to find out what happens if you put people into these positions and give them a task to do in which each has a piece of information which is essential for the completion of the task. Leavitt devised an ingenious experimental setting for this purpose. Five subjects sat round a table; they were separated from one another by partitions radiating out from the middle of the table. In the partitions there were slots which could be open or closed through which messages could be passed, and in the structure in the middle of the table there were also slots so that messages could be sent across the table if necessary. By opening some slots and closing others the four different systems of communication were provided.

The subjects were each given a card on which were five out of a possible six sets of simple symbols. One symbol was common to all cards, and a different symbol was missing from each of them. The problem was to find out which symbol was the common one. The subjects also each had six switches before him, each switch labelled with a symbol; when he thought he knew which symbol was the correct answer he threw the appropriate switch. The task was obviously correctly performed when all subjects threw the right switch, and incorrectly performed when one or more switches were wrongly thrown.

In the 'Y' and 'wheel' systems the subjects soon learnt to send information to C for analysis and to await his instructions. In the 'chain' it took rather longer to reach a scheme of procedure, but usually information went from both ends to C. From the 'circle', in which everybody could send messages in both directions, no consistent organization emerged.

The results are very much in the direction one would have predicted. So far as speed goes each system varied a good deal, but if one takes the fastest correct trial the 'Y' and the 'wheel' are significantly better than the 'circle' and the 'chain'. Members of the 'circle' naturally sent more messages to one another than was the case in the other three. The 'circle' also made more mistakes, but it is noticeable that a higher proportion of their mistakes were corrected than was the case with the others.

After the experiment the subjects were asked whether their group had a leader, and if so which one it was. In the 'circle' there was no unanimity, but as one passed from the 'chain' to the 'Y' to the 'wheel' one found increasing unanimity that C was the leader, and in all cases except the 'circle' C sent significantly more messages than the other, in increasing proportion in the familiar order: 'chain', 'Y', and 'wheel'. It is worth noting that this dominating position of C in the 'Y' and the 'wheel' was readily recognized in the course of interaction. In the 'wheel' particularly, the peripheral members had nothing to do but communicate with C and receive communications from him; C need not send any information, only the results of his analysis of the information he has received. Thus, if he makes a mistake all except one of the others is likely to make a mistake. He gets all the information first – and so he does in the 'Y' and nearly always in the 'chain'. He has the most complete independence; information pours in to him from all sides. No wonder he enjoyed himself. When asked about this, the peripheral members in the 'Y' and 'wheel' rated their enjoyment low, the central figure, on the other hand, rated his high, so did D in the 'Y' system. In the 'circle', however, where they were all in the same boat, no one having a natural flow of information towards him, they were confused about organizing a plan of campaign, but they all enjoyed themselves enormously.

We have here, indeed, a clear-cut conflict between efficiency and enjoyment which we must discuss in the next chapter. Efficiency, however, is not confined to the 'wheel'. Christie, Luce, and Macy[6] report a situation in which the 'circle' comes into its own. Instead of symbols, they used sets of differently coloured marbles. All went as expected when the marbles were of a clearly describable colour; when however they were changed for marbles of a cloudy and ambiguous coloration, the central figure was foxed. The peripheral members sent information which was not easy to organize, they were used to leaving everything to the 'leader', they were bored, they were not used to making comparisons because they received very little information. Not so the members of the 'circle', who were on the alert and were each of them used to getting information passed on to them. They soon realized that something was up.

This ingenious experiment is, of course, only a first move towards the experimental investigation of communication patterns. The setting is, as has already been said, remote from real life situations; only one factor, namely structure, is varied and the participants were not aware of the 'shape' of their network before they started. What emerges is a highlighting of the significance of differential spread of information in giving status to the person who has most of it, the readiness with which a routine is set up, and the relative attractions of systems in which all participate equally as compared with those in which participation is unequal.

Patterns of Interaction. The problem here is to discover some means of following a discussion in order to see whether there are any systematic uniformities which display themselves from one discussion to another. Anyone whose walk of life takes him to endless meetings will be inclined to think that this is a hopeless task. The only thing they might seem to have in common is their power to induce varying degrees of stultifying boredom. Even those who enjoy indulging in discussion will surely say that each session is quite different from any other. The personalities differ, the atmospheres differ, the topics differ; how can there be any uniformities?

All this is true, and the experiments, or rather observations, we are about to discuss concern only a narrow range of discussion and generalizations cannot be made to cover all types. Nevertheless, what emerges is undoubtedly of general interest and brings out features in discussions which are of importance and often miss the attention they deserve.

The outstanding figure in this kind of research is Robert F. Bales, and the key work is a book with the formidable title of *Interaction Process Analysis*,[7] published in 1950. The type of interaction process which Bales and his colleagues investigate is discussion on what they call a 'full-fledged' problem. This is a problem which the members of the group want to solve, which has a number of alternative solutions, either with respect to the problem as a whole or with respect to alternative steps which may be suggested as leading to a final decision, and in the solution of which the members will have to understand the problem, make suggestions about its solution, weigh up these suggestions, and decide on an agreed policy. Thus we have 'orientation' towards the solution of the task, suggestions as to a solution, the 'evaluation' of these suggestions, and decision-making, the acceptance or rejection of a proposal. However, as we shall see, more happens in the course of a discussion than that, and it is in this further analysis that Bales' contribution is of significance.

The first problem is to devise a schedule of categories of interaction which is at once small enough for the observer, who has to pigeon-hole the responses of the members of the group, to handle, and large enough to cover what are believed to be significant differences. This kind of methodological problem is, of course, nothing new. Anyone who is going to watch any kind of interaction process, in order to get some numerical measure of what occurs, must first decide on the classification of behaviour he is going to use. Studies of children, for instance, in which the observer wants to compare aggressive behaviour with co-operative behaviour or behaviour denoting indifference has to decide firstly what categories are going to be used, and secondly how they are to be defined so that the pigeon-holing is clear, not only to himself, but to anyone else who wants to repeat the investigation. It is difficult enough when one is dealing with little boys alternately fighting, playing together, and taking umbrage, but when it comes to people talking the difficulties are multiplied. They have been tackled by others as well as Bales. Carr[8] in 1929 made an attempt at analysing the interaction process when students were discussing how to spend their leisure time in the immediate future, while more recently Steinzer[9] has worked out a system of categories, having in mind an analysis of the intention of the speaker. This naturally has to be inferred from what is actually said, and work has been done with Steinzer's scheme on scripted records of discussions.

The system devised by Bales, however, has become the most important one because of the interest attaching to the results which have been achieved by means of it. The scheme is reproduced on page 131, and we must now consider one or two features of its mysterious symmetry.

In the first place it will be seen from the brackets on the left-hand side of the diagram that the twelve categories fall into two

SOCIAL-
EMOTIONAL
AREA:
POSITIVE

A

1 *Shows solidarity*, raises other's status, gives help, reward:

2 *Shows tension release*, jokes, laughs, shows satisfaction:

3 *Agrees*, shows passive acceptance, understands, concurs, complies:

TASK
AREA:
NEUTRAL

B

4 *Gives suggestion*, direction, implying autonomy for other:

5 *Gives opinion*, evaluation, analysis, expresses feeling, wish:

6 *Gives orientation*, information, repeats, clarifies, confirms:

C

7 *Asks for orientation*, information, repetition, confirmation:

8 *Asks for opinion*, evaluation, analysis, expression of feeling:

9 *Asks for suggestion*, direction, possible ways of action:

SOCIAL-
EMOTIONAL
AREA:
NEGATIVE

D

10 *Disagrees*, shows passive rejection, formality, withholds help:

11 *Shows tension*, asks for help, withdraws out of field:

12 *Shows antagonism*, deflates other's status, defends or asserts self:

a b c d e f

Key:

a Problems of Communication
b Problems of Evaluation
c Problems of Control
d Problems of Decision
e Problems of Tension Reduction
f Problems of Reintegration

A Positive Reactions
B Attempted Answers
C Questions
D Negative Reactions

main classes: those in the middle, 4–9, being concerned with the task itself and those at the two ends, 1, 2, 3, and 10, 11, 12, with emotional responses. These two major areas are subdivided into two in each case: 4, 5, and 6 are concerned with giving information, opinion, and suggestions; 7, 8, and 9 with asking for information, opinion, and suggestions; 1, 2, and 3 are categories implying what Bales calls 'positive' emotional responses, while 10, 11, and 12 imply what he calls 'negative' responses. Secondly, the categories can be taken in pairs, as will be seen on the right-hand side of the diagram: 6 and 7 deal with 'orientation', such as setting out the problem and giving factual information; 5 and 8 are concerned with evaluation such as 'Have we done this, that, or the other?' or 'We ought to make sure that . . .', anything, in fact, that indicates an appraisal of the issues which have to be faced; 4 and 9 are described as being concerned with 'control'. This is an odd word to find here. The statements which come under this are statements such as: 'I think we ought to do so and so' or 'Has anybody an idea as to what we ought to do about this?' Suggestions, in fact. The word 'control', however, is not lightly used. In Bales' view a definite suggestion, as distinct from an appraisal of an issue, is a kind of invitation to the rest of the party to commit themselves, and thereby to limit their range of future choice. In this sense it is implicitly an act of 'control', and as such is liable to be faintly resented, giving rise to tension in the emotion sectors. The categories 3 and 10 are decisions to accept or reject; 2 and 11 are purely emotional responses. In an example given by Bales a member is observed sighing heavily, and examining his fingernails; this is scored as 11. In the same example a man is supposed to make a rather offensive remark directed at another member; this is scored as 12, but the laughter that followed is scored as 2. This is an instance of one of the major principles underlying the whole scheme, namely that if the group is to remain in being, such hostilities and disagreements as are aroused must be counteracted by positive emotional release, re-establishing friendliness. Finally 1 and 12, which have already been mentioned, are described as being concerned with 'problems of integration', rather more definite than mere laughter on the positive side and disruptive on the negative side.

Although Bales gives instructions about what kinds of remarks should come under which categories, it must be admitted that considerable practice and experience are required before the scheme can be used effectively, and even with experience there are many borderline cases. This, of course, sets limits to the practical utility of the scheme.

And now, as to the way in which it is used: the observer has a chart on which he registers the category of statement (or gesture) made, who makes it, and to whom it is addressed, whether to another person or to the group as a whole. It should be remarked here that the groups had no official chairman, to whom or through whom all remarks are addressed. The information is used to construct three measures: first there is the 'profile' which represents the percentage of each category found in the total number of reactions made; secondly there is the 'matrix' of interaction in which are shown the number of remarks made by each person, the number addressed to each person, and the number addressed to the group as a whole; thirdly there is a calculation of 'phase' difference, showing the change in proportions of the major groups of categories through the whole meeting.

'Profiles' fall into family groups according to the type of problem. Of course each 'profile' will differ in detail from every other, but if you compare profiles of people discussing a chess problem, they look different from those of people discussing a problem about human relations. The profiles are usually dealt with in groups, summed together, the argument being that if profiles of individual members differ from one another more than the total profiles for the series of groups differ among themselves, then there is some system at work. Taking problems about human relations as an example it is found that there is a tendency for about 50 per cent of the items to be 'initial acts', giving suggestions, opinions, and orientations; these are, indeed, 'attempted answers'. Now, as we have already hinted, in Bales' view an 'initial act' of this kind disturbs the equilibrium of the group and a response has to be made. The group has *two* tasks: coming to an agreement on a solution, and preserving the group intact. Of the remaining 50 per cent you have about 25 per cent 'positive reactions', of agreement and consolidation – after all, the group is there to reach agreement. These items are thought of as bringing the disturbance to an end. Of the remaining 25 per cent, about 12 per cent are negative reactions which tend to precipitate further attempted answers which start the cycle again. Of the rest, about 6 per cent are questions and about 7 per cent responses to questions in the form of attempted answers which are not initiating but reactions to the questions.

These proportions have in fact been found, according to Bales, recurring from one set of instances to another. We need not, however, necessarily take the actual proportions seriously, though their recurrence is odd enough. What is interesting is the conception of a discussion as a field of tension in which two forces are at work: a force directed towards the performance of a task, and a force directed towards the maintenance of some kind of equilibrium.

The 'matrices' reveal the amount of participation of each member, and the direction of his and other members' remarks. We have already noticed that as a group increases in size the participation of one member becomes more and more important. This certainly happens with groups of six members, with no official leader. Further interesting regularities are found. The most active member addresses the group as a whole more than anyone else, and he receives more interaction from all the others, including the least active. Furthermore everyone seems to address other people roughly in proportion to their rank in productivity. The most productive will tend to address and be addressed by the next most productive, and the least productive will say but little to one another. Out of a total of inter-individual remarks of 12,205, in one aggregate matrix, No. 1 addressed No. 2 1,238 times and was addressed by No. 2 1,748 times, while No. 5 only addressed 28 remarks to No. 6, and received 44 remarks from him.

Since most of the initiating acts are orientation, appraisals, and suggestions which prompt question or agreement or disagreement, it is not surprising that the most productive member gets most responses, while the man who is not productive gets but few. Indeed in the *individual* profiles, the productive man scores on 'initial acts', while the less productive scores most on positive and negative reactions. It all seems rather familiar, but it is gratifying to see the familiar emerging in this somewhat artificial contest.

Further confirmation that high-ranking initiators receive more communications from low-rankers is to be found in the artificially devised high and low status groups in Kelley's experiment described on p. 42. It will be remembered that some groups were told that their job was important and would remain so, others that it was important but that they might have to do something less important, others that their job was unimportant and would remain so, and, finally, others that their job was unimportant but that they might be moved up.

More messages were sent by the low non-mobile groups to the higher ones, and they contained more material which was irrelevant to the task. Kelley suggests that this is due to an attempt to escape from their relatively unpleasant position, and also, perhaps, as a kind of substitute for their lack of real mobility.

The evidence also supports Homans' hypothesis that the higher a member's rank the larger the number of persons who originate interaction with him.

The process in time is interesting.[10] If you divide the whole meeting, or aggregate of meetings, into three phases of equal duration you find that orientation progressively declines, evaluation remains high, positive reactions go up, negative reactions go up in the second phase and rise slightly in the third, and 'control' rises continuously. Suggestions give rise to faint hostility, these negative responses are further increased in the middle, perhaps, by a feeling that 'we are getting nowhere'. Towards the end, too, there is a pressure to accept a decision, which, as we have seen, Bales suggests is faintly unpleasing. Right at the end the positive categories 1, 2, and 3 rise high. As Bales puts it 'the successfully recovering group tends to confine its agreement and to release in diffuse ways the tension built up in its prior task efforts, repairing the damage done to its state of consensus and social integration',[11] and so the group breaks up in a gale of laughter and a whirl of back-slapping (Category 1).

All these results are expressed in quantitative terms: the number of statements of certain categories or the number of communications between one person and another. There are also certain qualitative results which are of interest, and which link the theme of this chapter with that of the next.

After the discussion meetings, Bales[12] asked who contributed the best ideas, who did most to guide the discussion, and 'Whom do you like or dislike?' The first two correlated fairly highly with rank in initiation of ideas. The person who talks most is regarded as the most productive. We all know to our cost that this is by no means always so, but it is intelligible that in a quasi-experimental situation in which the subjects are expected to talk, the very fact of talking is likely to carry prestige. This, too, is cumulative. A person who is deemed to be productive at one meeting is expected to be productive at the next, and this is likely to heighten his confidence and loquacity.

The advantage of loquacity is brought out by an odd piece of research carried out by Strodtbeck.[13] He compared husband-wife interaction among the Mormons, the Texans, and the Navaho Indians. The husband and wife were asked to make some evaluation of an experience they both shared. Of course they differed and were then confronted with the discrepancies and invited to reconcile them. Among the Mormons, the husband tended to win, among the Navahos it was the wife, while among the Texans it was about fifty-fifty. This difference is put down to the different status of husband and wife in the different cultures, but it was noticed that the one who was victorious was the one who talked most. While it is to be hoped that a general interest in social psychology will become widespread, it might be disastrous if all its findings were put to practical usage.

To return to Bales. After the first of a series of meetings the most productive member was also the most liked; he had, one might say, got them out of their difficulties in an unusual situation. However, after a series of meetings, when the group had settled down to its task, the one judged most productive became the least liked. One of his subjects felt this so much that he dropped his productive role. This is an instance of the ambiguous position of the leader. He may score high on productivity, but his very productivity is felt as 'control' and he therefore arouses an element of dislike in his group. This fits also with the Homans hypothesis that if a person initiates interaction with another more than the other does with him, the latter will develop an attitude of respect (and possibly hostility) towards the former. Liking in this situation seems to go towards the second or third rank in productivity; there is a tendency to choose upward, but not too far up. In some groups, such as the Street Corner Gang studied by Whyte, the leader safeguards his position by working through lieutenants. This is familiar enough. The general, the colonel, the vice-chancellor, and the gang leaders are all potential targets of hostility; from them comes control. They delegate the more unpleasant tasks to their staff, who bear the brunt of immediate animosity, and occasionally buy a little popularity by using a prerogative of mercy.

The point of Bales' work, as we have said, lies in his examination of the tensions which develop in a relatively simple task situation. He does not enter into the underlying currents of suspicion and safeguarding of positions in the way that Jaques did when he investigated the stresses and strains of the Glacier Metal factory.[14] He is concerned rather with the inevitable alternatives of task work and emotional release. His situations are simple. There is no chairman, there are no official statements, the air is not, as in most committees, loud with the sound of the grinding of axes. In real life situations all these factors complicate the situation. Information is distorted by self-interest; communication is hindered because of possible remote consequences and immediate inferences; people have to be cajoled, delicately handled and so forth because of their sensitivity or pride of rank or because of their power. At the same time, besides all these complications, there may well be certain very general processes which are to be found in all 'fully-fledged' discussions, and it is with these that Bales is concerned.

We have so far, in this chapter and in the one that preceded it, been concerned with the output of groups. We have, in the last few paragraphs, considered the likes and dislikes which develop in group activity. In the next chapter these will be considered rather more fully.

CHAPTER 9

EXPERIMENTAL GROUPS

III: Group Structures

EVERY group, as has already been said, involves emotional relations of like and dislike among its members, it develops norms of its own, and it develops a hierarchy of prestige often culminating in a single person who has a dominating influence. Furthermore groups differ in their cohesiveness and in the degree to which all members participate in its activities. These features make up what is meant by its 'structure'.

Homans, it will be remembered, distinguishes between the 'external' and the 'internal' systems. The 'external' system is determined by the environment in the widest sense of the word, including the demands made by the environment in calling the group into being. It is concerned with what the group has to do to perpetuate itself in the environment. If it is there to discuss, then there are certain things that have to be done for discussion to proceed; if to play a game, to engage in some industrial occupation, to establish itself as a procreative, continuous entity, or merely to provide friendly intercourse among its members, the 'task', if we may call it so, determines its structure from what might be considered an external point of view. When, however, a group has been brought together, and its members have interacted for a while, a kind of additional 'internal' structure develops. Friendships are formed, rules of conduct over and above those required by the overt purpose of the group make themselves felt, prestige is accorded to some more than to others, some get bored and some do not.

This distinction between the 'external' and 'internal' systems, or, perhaps, it would be better expressed as 'external' and 'internal' aspects of groups, is one that is frequently denoted by the contrast made between 'formal' organization and 'informal' organization. A good deal of the literature on industrial psychology is nowadays concerned with pointing out the significance of the informal developments which occur within the formal setting. It is pointed out, and rightly so, that we ignore the informal relationships at our peril, when alterations in the formal organization are contemplated. Some seating accommodation, the position near a window, a fire, or a door, may be informally invested with values, and changes which ignore such values are liable to give rise to irritation. How much more then is it likely to be the case when normative rules, prestige hierarchies, and other group values are disturbed without a word of explanation.

From a somewhat different point of view, but closely related to all this, Jennings[1] has distinguished the 'socio-group' and the 'psyche-group'. The 'socio-group' is one in which there is association for work or for living and is founded on a 'collective criterion'; the 'psyche-group' is based on association for private satisfaction in the association's activities, and in it the 'uniqueness of the individual as a personality is appreciated and allowed for, with varying degrees of spontaneous indulgence and affection'. The distinction here is between groups in which the task is emphasized, and those in which the pleasure of personal intercourse is emphasized. Looked at like this, the two types of group become limiting ends of a continuum; at one end we picture a group with scarcely any recognition of the personalities of its members, who are completely preoccupied with the job on which they are engaged, while at the other end of the scale is a group doing nothing but bask in the enjoyment of companionship. Between these extremes are, we would say, the groups of real life, in which sometimes the one aspect, sometimes the other, is important.

This distinction paves the way for another of practical importance. Chester Barnard,[2] using regrettably confusing language, points out that a group may be judged on two standards: it may be more or less 'effective' in the performance of its task, and more or less 'efficient' in the personal rewards it provides to its members. Obviously we would be inclined to change the adjectives round, and in this book, when 'efficiency' is referred to, it will mean being good at the job, and not necessarily affording pleasure to the participants of an interpersonal nature. The distinction between these two types of assessment, however, is of practical importance because, as has been indicated, the pleasures and unpleasures of personal intercourse in a group are frequently neglected, and also because there is a widespread view nowadays that if you increase the amount of enjoyable personal intercourse, you automatically make the group more 'efficient', in our sense.

This is by no means necessarily the case, on a short-term view, anyway. If people enjoy working together they may very well spend a good deal of their time gossiping, or even combining to defeat the purposes of the external bodies who have called the group into being. In the long run, however, it may, on occasion, be prudent to sacrifice a certain amount of efficiency in order that solidarity should be preserved. Somehow or other a balance has to be struck between a degree of efficiency which proves frustrating, particularly to the peripheral members, and a degree of matiness that turns a working group into a jolly picnic on the beach.

The interference of production by social intercourse has, for instance, been noted by Horsfall and Arensberg[3] in an industrial situation; they found that of 4 groups of 7, the least productive were those who chatted most among themselves.

Let us turn now to a closer inspection of the structure of groups as revealed by experimental inquiry.

If we disregard the rather pedantic but not entirely ridiculous notion that each individual with his internal conversations is a group, then the smallest group is the pair. The German sociologist Simmel[4] directed his subtle analytical mind to the peculiarities of pairs. If they persist the individualities of each member get fuller expression than is the case with a larger number, and the death or departure of one of the members destroys the group altogether. It is in the pair relationship that the sharing of specific experience reaches its height, and a certain weight of responsibility is placed upon each of the participants to keep the group intact—there is, in fact no group, 'outside' the individual members, to blame for anything that goes wrong.

The presence of a third is notoriously interruptive. Each member of the original pair is likely to have a different relationship to the third, and so the triad tends to shift into three pairs: A B, B C,

A C, with one left out. A fourth and a fifth make less difference to a triad than a third added to a pair.

The plight of the 'odd man out' has been experimentally investigated by Mills,[5] who studied 48 three-person groups making up a story round three ambiguous pictures used in a thematic apperception test. They all seemed to divide themselves into two who interacted a great deal and one who contributed less. Mills further points out that in many situations the disturbing presence of a third person may consolidate a pair in opposition to him.

Leaving aside the peculiarities of pairs and triads, it is worth pointing out that the members of groups may either be strangers to one another or they may be friends or enemies already. The initial stages of group activity will obviously be influenced by such considerations. If, for instance, they are friends, communication is likely to be easy from the start. Assuming that all parties are equally interested in doing whatever it is they have to do, initial friendship is clearly advantageous, and it has been found that putting people who like one another to work together increases efficiency.[6] They are also more likely to be able to resist frustration.

An instance of groups in frustrating situations has been investigated by French.[7] He compared the responses to frustration on the part of groups already organized and known to one another with those of groups of strangers. They were given insoluble problems to solve. Among the members of the organized groups there was considerable participation all round, and a strong degree of solidarity. The unorganized groups hardly achieved any solidarity to speak of; they tended to split into factions, and several members never got a word in. The significant point, however, is that the organized group displayed much more intra-group aggression than did the unorganized group. The solidarity of the group was sufficient to allow of this without impairment.

Two other findings emerged from French's experiment, which included as its final episode an alarming trick. When the groups had finished their problem solving they were asked to fill in a questionnaire. The experimenter then pretended he had an engagement and left them to it, secretly locking the door as he went away. This was the signal for the release of smoke under a door leading into an adjoining room. To make matters more realistic a siren was sounded, and all the time the groups were being watched through a one-way screen in the ceiling. The groups behaved in different ways. Some were taken in and were alarmed, others were sceptical and smelt a rat as well as the smoke. However, as in the frustration situation, so here, all members of organized groups tended to react in the same way: either they were all frightened or all sceptical. This was not nearly so apparent with the unorganized groups. The other point was that the organized groups who were frightened were more frightened than the unorganized men, and more vigorous in their reactions.

French explains all this in terms of 'Field Theory'; the power field of the group was stronger in the organized than in the unorganized group. We may suppose that if, in the fear situation, the organized groups had been drilled for danger they might have shown greater coolness than the unorganized men; as it was those who were afraid were more afraid. It would appear from this that in a dangerous situation, membership of an organized group might afford very inadequate protection.

Undoubtedly, too, people differ at a very early age in their tendency to dominate others. It is reasonable to suppose that this is related to innate qualities of forcefulness and energy, but as usual a caveat has to be entered against making assumptions of this kind. The power to influence others, and the tendency to make the attempt are clearly influenced by individual life-histories and by cultural standards. A potentially vigorous individual may be brought up to give orders and assume that other people will obey them. It is obvious that class differences play an important part in power relations, defined in this way, between persons of different classes. Again, as we shall see, whatever their physiological or mental abilities, or whatever their skills, people may acquire influence by being good at whatever it may be that is admired.

Once they get together, however, it soon becomes clear to all concerned who is important and who is not. The attribution and acceptance of influence was studied by Lippitt[8] and his colleagues in two types of children's camps, one for disturbed children of a low socio-economic level, and one for normal boys of middle-class origin. They studied what they call 'contagion', and deliberate attempts at influence. By 'contagion' they mean doing what another person is doing without any attempt on the part of the other person to make one do it. They found a clear distinction between those who had power and those who had not. This was agreed to by all, with respect to themselves and to the others. In general the lower-powered children were influenced by contagion from the higher-powered ones, and accepted more directions from them. The high-powered children knew what their position was, and were in fact more socially active than the others. In the middle-class camp, however, there was more reciprocity, and the high-powered boys were not more directive in their attempts to influence the others. In both camps it was in socially directive activity that the high-powered members excelled rather than in mere impulsiveness.

The point here is that power relations soon get established and are recognized by the holders of power and by the others.

Using Homans' concept of the 'external' system, we have seen that this determines at the outset how much, and what kind of, interaction there will be. We have noted his hypothesis that the more interaction there is between people, the more they will tend to like one another. Although there are limits to this, as Homans recognizes, it does appear that interaction draws people together, not only into physical proximity, but also into some kind of emotional relationship. There is nothing odd about this when we consider the need everyone has acquired from infancy to be liked, because signs of liking are signs of worth and goodness, and have been taken to be signs that needs will be satisfied. The result is that we all tend to ingratiate ourselves, and give signs of goodwill to other people. Out of this grow shared experiences, the memory of which further consolidates the group. The very demeanour of the person who refuses to join in may be taken as evidence of the pressure to do so. Of course there are plenty of resistances to interaction itself. We have our cult of privacy, we fear rebuffs, and we may not be sure what we shall be let in for, but even in the short space of a railway journey, when there is a delay on the lines and conversational interaction is inaugurated, a sense of friendliness almost always develops.

No doubt this is most in evidence, as Susan Isaacs has pointed out, when there is a target for collective hostility: the old trout in the corner who will keep opening (or closing) the window. Undoubtedly contrasting rank lends solidarity, as when the executive officers, or the clerical staff, or the workers on the shop floor, who interact with one another more than they interact with other members of the enterprise, are, in addition, segregated by rank from other groups. At the same time it is arguable that in the absence of a hostile 'out-group', and in the absence of a contrasting group of lower or higher rank, the very process of interaction itself induces friendliness.

Homans illustrates his hypothesis by reference to the bank-wiring cliques described on page 52. When Sherif divided his boys into two groups, the final sociometric assessment showed that choices which had originally been scattered about the group as a whole were now directed within the sub-group. To take one more instance, Bovard,[9] who compared 'leader-centred' groups in which interaction between members was discouraged with 'group-centred' ones, in which interaction was encouraged, found that there was greater liking among the members of the latter type of group than among the members of the former.

Besides the liking which grows up among equals because they are all in the same boat together, we shall find further sources of liking when we come to the development of a hierarchy.

Before dealing with that, however, we must consider the establishment of group norms. It has already been pointed out (p. 12) that normativeness as such is a prerequisite for continuous interaction. The interacting parties must develop a mutually agreed system of expectation in accordance with which the action of the individual is geared to the reaction of the others, and theirs, in turn, to his response. What expectations, what rules, will be precipitated will clearly depend partly on the general culture within which the participants have been brought up, partly by the 'external system', and partly by the 'internal system' which develops within it. The normative regulation of the 'internal system' will be partly determined by the attitudes, the fears, and the ambitions of the persons concerned with respect to the demands of the situation.

Thus there are certain general ways in which workmen are expected to behave to one another. When they are on a job there are good ways and bad ways of doing it, and there are almost certainly rules imposed by an external authority which have to be observed. Within the group itself informal customs and regulations in addition to those imposed by the task itself will certainly develop. What these will be will depend in part on whether the members of the group identify themselves with the standards of the 'external system' or not. Among the bank-wirers, for example, there developed, apparently without any discussion on the matter, a restrictive standard of output. They were afraid, perhaps irrationally, that if they raised their output the rates would be cut, while if they lowered it they might get the sack.

On the other hand, it is perfectly possible, and indeed frequently happens, that a group should identify itself with the demands of the 'external system' and incorporate what one might call the official norms into their own informal ones. In this case what in Communist countries is called the 'model worker' is, indeed, accepted as a model; in the other situation he would be blackguarded in language which is scarcely printable.

The pressure to conform has already been illustrated by examples of what has been called the 'levelling' process, by which extremes are avoided so that there is a convergence to a mean.

An extreme case of the influence of group pressure is to be found in an experiment carried out by Asch.[10] His subjects were invited to match the length of a given line with one of three unequal lines. The groups consisted of eight persons, and the judgements were given aloud. Seven of the members of the groups, however, had been put up by the experimenter to agree on a judgement which was quite clearly wrong. The unfortunate naïve subject was thus faced with a group that violated the evidence of his senses. What was he to do? In the majority of cases, it is true, the naïve subjects followed their own judgement against the majority, but many of them showed acute embarrassment in doing so. A third of them, however, yielded to pressure, a few saying that

145

they saw the lines as the majority 'saw' them, most of them saying that they thought their own perception must be wrong and therefore followed the majority, while the rest thought the majority wrong, but did not like to differ from them.

The pressure of the group may not only, albeit in rare cases, make a person depart from his better judgement of objects perceived in front of him; it may daunt a vigorous and domineering character. Merei,[11] for instance, in his experiments in a nursery school noted, as many have before him, that some children are dominating and others rather ineffectual. He collected the ineffectual ones together into groups and, sure enough, they developed a set of institutions among themselves with regard to seating arrangements, playing arrangements, rituals and so on. Then he introduced one of the forceful little characters into these microcosms. The interloper was defeated by tradition.

This by no means meant that his forcefulness went by the board. What happened was that he accepted the rules and then dominated the situation in terms of them, either as a giver of orders, or as a 'diplomat', accepting the main rules, but modifying the details.

From this experiment in the force of tradition Merei draws a conclusion of some interest. The weaklings, as we may call them, were completely dominated by the stronger characters in the general rough and tumble of nursery-school life. When they were bound together they acquired collective strength. Indeed there were those who started giving orders, and continued to do so, even when the more forceful personalities arrived. 'The strength of the group', says Merei, 'strengthens its members.'

The norms of the group are preserved by punishment and persuasion, by activities, that is to say, calculated to make the deviate toe the line. In the bank-wiring group the man who worked too fast was condemned as a 'rate-buster', the one who was too slow as the 'chiseler', while extreme deviance was met with a sharp blow on the arm, called 'binging'. In Whyte's Street Corner Gang, an accepted rank order of proficiency in playing bowls was one of the norms. A member who ranked low on other grounds might be good at bowls and might defeat players who had defeated high rankers in his gang, but when he played against a gang high-ranker, he was seldom 'on form'; if he did play as well as he could, he was liable to be barracked. The extreme forms of social control are ostracism, expulsion, and, in certain cases, death.

Less extreme measures may be applied in dealing with the deviate in a discussion group. Schachter[12] carried out an extremely elaborate experiment in which he used planted deviates. He had thirty-two groups of five to seven members, and divided them into four types, on the basis of whether the members had expressed interest in the topic suggested for discussion or not, and according to whether the subject actually discussed was relevant to the purpose of the meeting or not. The topics were fictitiously related to real life. Some were told, for example, that a group of judges and social workers really wanted their views on the treatment of delinquents, or that a new national magazine was being started, and that advice was wanted about the type of material to be published in it. The 'high cohesive' groups were made up of those who discussed, or started to discuss, the topic in which they had expressed interest, the 'low cohesive' groups were made up of those who had expressed lack of interest in the topic they were told to discuss. The factor of relevance was introduced by letting the groups go on discussing the subject they started on, whether they liked it or not, or introducing another subject altogether. Thus he got combinations of 'high' and 'low' cohesion with 'relevance' and 'irrelevance' making his four types of groups. Into each he introduced a 'deviate' who persistently disagreed, a 'slider' who started by disagreeing and then yielded to pressure, and a 'model' character who followed the majority view.

During the experiments in all cases more communication was directed to the deviate than to the 'slider' or the 'model' men. In the 'high cohesive' group, who continued to discuss the topic of their choice, this concentration of communication on to the deviate rose to a peak during the meeting, and then fell to a point which betokened ostracism. The slider was attacked until he slid, after which not much attention was paid to him. Few communications were addressed to the man who agreed with the majority. All this was much less marked among the 'low cohesive' groups, and especially among those who were made to discuss a subject quite irrelevant to the purpose of their meeting, which bored them anyway.

Not unnaturally, when a sociometric assessment was asked for after the meetings, the deviate scored very low among those who were interested in the subject and wearied of his consistent disagreement, whereas he was not markedly rejected by those who were not in the least interested in what they were supposed to discuss.

The experiment is a good example of methodological ingenuity. It brings out the important, even though fairly obvious, relationship between interest in or concern with an activity and reaction to the person who persistently differs from the rest of the group. The more insistent and urgent the task is felt to be, the more efforts will be made first to convert the nonconformist, then to cold-shoulder him.

Prestige. The establishment of norms, provided they are strongly felt, plays an important part in the allocation of prestige, to which subject we must now turn.

Most of the work on small groups in laboratories is of necessity concerned with informal ranking, but in real life there are three factors which determine prestige: formal, semi-formal, and informal. By 'formal' factors are meant those rankings which constitute the official power structure. In offices and industrial establishments, in schools and universities, in the services and in the church, there are official hierarchies of office, each with its sphere of competence and responsibility, frequently distinguished by dress, badges, or some other ornamental device, or by the softness of the chair in which they are entitled to sit, or the size and texture of the carpet upon which their underlings stand. They are usually segregated for the purposes of eating and drinking, and they usually have separate lavatories of differential grandeur. Such trivial marks of distinction are particularly necessary to bolster up prestige when, as alas! sometimes happens, it is divorced from skill.

The word 'trivial' has been used, but let no one think that such distinctions are unimportant to those that benefit by them.

A man may walk miles to wash his hands in the 'right' basin, and anyone who has ever been concerned with the marshalling of a procession or with determining eligibility for club membership will be only too aware of the susceptibilities of which he has to take account.

The formal system of prestige is familiar enough to everyone. The semi-formal order is rather less obvious. There is frequently a hierarchy among employees which may or may not be marked by differential wages, and which is by no means clearly recognized by the outside world. The men who wired connectors, in the bank-wiring study, were thought a cut above the men who wired selectors, though to the uninitiated they seemed to be doing much the same thing. In a study of restaurants in America, Whyte[13] found that the male cooks were superior in rank to the waitresses, the person who handled beans was not allowed to touch the salad, and the peeler of potatoes must not go so far above his station as to slice them for frying. In many large shops it is grander to sell in one department than in another, and so forth. And not only in the world of paid employment do we find such semi-formal distinctions; in prison the safe-breaker is superior in rank to the pickpocket or the bag-snatcher, and bitterly resents being classed with them as a mere breaker of the law.

These formal and semi-formal occupational hierarchies form a framework within which the informal prestige scheme develops. When the three schemes overlap, sometimes the informal prestige hierarchy conflicts, and sometimes agrees with the other two.

Informal prestige is accorded on a basis of what the group deems to be 'good' behaviour, and clearly this will depend upon the purposes of the group. In so far as they are concentrating on their task, it will be given to those who are productive and helpful; in so far as they are concerned with companionship, marks will be given to those who are companionable; in so far as they are interested in attitudes, those who display the approved ones will rank highest. It may happen that different people have high ranks on different schemes of marking, it often happens that a person with a high rank on one criterion will have a high rank on another. This, indeed, is what Jennings[14] found. She noted that girls in the school she worked in often chose the same ones for working with and for living with. The tendency to diffuse admiration has also been noted by Bales in his discussion groups. Anyone who is productive on one occasion is expected to do well on others.

This is, of course, in accord with everyday experience; the admired expert in one field is expected to be an expert in every other. Sometimes, unhappily, he, or she, seems to accept the imputation.

There do, however, seem to be two kinds of criteria which do not always go together. These are measures of popularity and measures of excellence. We have seen that on work and living-with choice in Jennings' material there was considerable overlap among what she calls the 'over-chosens', but when the criterion of choice was 'With whom would you like to spend your leisure time?' the overlap with the other criteria was by no means so marked. It was this, indeed, that led to the distinction between the 'socio-group' and the 'psyche-group'. It seems, however, that the more often a girl was chosen on the work and living-together criterion, the more often was her choice on leisure-time reciprocated. One sees, perhaps, a tendency for people to choose those equal in rank to themselves for their personal friends. Furthermore, the leisure-time groups are smaller than the other ones and therefore more selectivity is at work.

We obviously choose our friends on a variety of grounds: for their appearance, their wit, their charm and so on. One powerful factor, however, is the degree to which they share our standards of opinion and moral outlook. It is not surprising therefore to find that in many cases sociometric choice is found to go with other accepted standards of excellence. Among the bank-wirers the most popular man was the one who acted up to the norms of the group most conscientiously. In his study of Bennington College, where a liberal tradition of thought had been established, Newcomb[15] found that the pressure of public opinion changed the attitude of the students as they passed through from their first year to their last, and that popularity, again, was connected with a display of liberal views.

The expectation that those you like will agree with you, and those you dislike will not, is illustrated by an experiment carried out by Horowitz and his colleagues.[16] They studied the friendship pattern of twenty subjects and then confronted them with three assertions which had been made during a discussion meeting, with the names of those who had uttered them. They then asked the members of the group to write down their own agreement or disagreement with the statements, and also who else they thought would agree or disagree. The upshot was that they agreed with statements made by their friends and disagreed with those made by people they liked less, and expected their friends to do the same.

In a curious study of the attitudes and relations of foremen and shop-stewards, Jacobson, Charters and Lieberman[17] found, as one would expect, that when foremen were asked how shop-stewards should behave, most of them said they should play a passive role, while most of the shop-stewards said they should be active. There were, however, a few foremen and a few shop-stewards who took the opposite view. Not unnaturally the 'deviant' foremen got on better with the shop-stewards and the 'deviant' shop-stewards got on better with foremen. They also found that when the shop-stewards failed to behave in an active way, they and the union they represented were rejected by the workers. If a foreman did not act in that kind of way, he was not thought the less of – it was not his job. If, however, he *did* act as a shop-steward should, he was highly praised for it.

This illustrates the complexity of judgement when you have a variety of roles. You are pleased with someone who furthers your interests whether he is expected to or not. If he does not further your interests, you resent it, if it is his job to do so, but not if his obligations lie elsewhere.

We should now look at the results of Thibaut's experiment with artificially produced ranking difference, described on page 43. It will be remembered that he got some boys to play games in which one role was more sought after than another, which was of a rather menial kind, like holding a target for the others to shy at. The experiment was extremely complicated and only the most general results will be considered. Some of the teams played the attractive part the whole time, others played the unattractive part the whole time. Before the experiment began, a sociometric assessment was made, and it was found, not unnaturally, that some boys were more popular than others. The teams were so made up as to include in each popular boys and less popular ones. After the whole experiment had been completed, another sociometric assessment was made to see whether the whole experience had made any difference. The high-ranking teams were drawn closer together. The most popular tended to choose one another rather than members of other teams, and the less popular tended to choose members of their own teams. In the consistently low ranking teams there was greater cohesiveness, derived no doubt from hostility towards the teams who always had the more attractive things to do, but the less popular members of the consistently low-ranking teams did not change their allegiance. They were just as likely to choose members of the other teams as before. This lack of cohesion among the less popular members of teams which continued to have the most boring things to do is no doubt due to their wretched plight. It was they who tried to escape from the torment altogether; they were not supported by a knowledge of their popularity, they were not encouraged by enjoyment of an attractive role; there were no grounds for solidarity with the other members of the team to develop.

Another source of liking, then, is not so much skill or excellence as the sharing of a common plight. This, however, is somewhat doubtful in its effect, because the unpleasantness of the situation is a force driving one away from it altogether.

We have so far considered group interaction and the likings, the norms, and the prestige rankings which it produces. Very generally it would appear that equals interacting together tend to like one another, that when rules are established a prestige ranking emerges, and on the whole popularity and excellence tend to go together. The ranking system, however, very frequently has a top-ranking member who acts as the leader.

Of recent years a great deal has been written about the importance of leadership. Attempts have been made to pin down the qualities which mark out the leader, and they have all failed. Further attempts have been made to analyse the functions of leadership, and these have been more successful. It would, however, be impossible to attempt to summarize all the literature on the subject. For our purposes only a few of the features of leadership will be discussed.

To begin with, the familiar distinction must be made between the formal and informal leader. The former is the office-holder with recognized authority within his sphere of competence; the latter is the group representative, the person who furthers the interests of the group, and who comes closest to their ideals in his behaviour. In perhaps the majority of cases the role of the formal leader is quite different from the role of the informal one, but it happens now and then in situations in which guidance has to be given that the informal leader usurps the position of the formal one. Furthermore, as we have already hinted, the predicaments of the two have characteristics in common.

With the appointment of the formal leader we are not explicitly concerned. We are more interested in the emergence of the informal leader. Since he embodies the norms of the group, and is there to further their interests, it is quite clear that no single quality or even set of qualities can be pointed to as qualities of leadership. It all depends on the group, and on the situations which confront it. All one can say is that a withdrawn, unsociable, and self-absorbed character is less likely to display leadership behaviour than others who have closer contact with their fellows, but even this is merely a matter of likelihood. After all, the most diffident, the most misanthropic, and the most self-centred of men may sometimes pluck up courage and show his companions the way, particularly if he is anxious to reach a destination.

Those social psychologists who concentrate on what actually happens in concrete situations naturally prefer to think in terms of acts of leadership. Thus Hemphill defines such acts in the following terms: 'To lead,' he says, 'is to engage in an act which initiates a structure in the interaction of others as part of the process of solving a mutual problem.'[18] This dissolves the 'leader' into his acts of leading, and serves to remind us that in many situations the leadership role switches from one person to another, that there may be, in fact, many leaders in the same group if one follows its course of interaction from one moment to another.

When we are considering so-called 'leaderless' groups, groups, that is to say, who have no official leader and no elected one, it is quite true that the initiation of activity is done sometimes by one person, sometimes by another. It is for this reason that the 'leaderless group' is used by selectors for official leadership positions. They watch the group attempting to solve a task, and note the combination of initiative and encouragement of others as it appears in the course of interaction.

The 'situational approach' to leadership is undoubtedly a valuable correction of the rather vague assumption that there are born leaders about the place, if only we could find them. In fact, however, as a group continues to exist, single individuals nearly always emerge who perform leadership-acts much more frequently than anyone else, who are not only required to 'initiate interaction' with other members of the group, but who are also looked up to as the group representative. In such cases it is not unreasonable to think of these individuals as 'leaders' even though they may not, at any given moment, be leading. The final test, of course, is whether they are accepted as such by their 'followers'.

As representative of the group the leader has more contact with other people outside the group. This was pointed out by Whyte in his account of the Street Corner Boys, and when Horsfall and Arensberg[19] investigated working teams in a shoe factory they found that those who had the greatest percentage of initiatory action as compared with responses, interacted more with members of other teams. A rather different feature of leadership comes out in that experiment of Sherif's, to which several references have been made, in which he divided the camp of boys into two groups, who became progressively more hostile to one another. The leaders of the groups were far less hostile towards the other gang than their followers.

The leader, then, must be a pattern of conduct, granted that he has not been appointed by an external body – and even then prestige of office may not outweigh gross departure from the conduct of its holder. Paradoxically enough, he also may have more licence in matters which do not form part of the group's system of values. On the other hand, the low ranking member does not feel the pressure to conform; his position does not depend upon it. Provided he acts up to the minimum required for acceptance by the group, he can afford to be otherwise disreputable because he can fall no further. This relative freedom from constraint of the low-ranking member is not confined to small face-to-face groups. In any society there are norms of conduct, and prestige goes to a large extent with acting up to such norms. The classes in a society who have prestige will feel the pressure of the norms much more forcibly than those who have none; it is up to their position to keep the rules. How often do we read of judges expressing shocked surprise when a 'gentleman' has kicked over the traces: 'With all your advantages . . .' they say. It is not surprising, therefore, that the majority of delinquents are to be found among the working classes, who have less of a stake in the prestige system.

As exemplar, then, the leader is bound by normative values, with certain areas of freedom. As representative, he enjoys a certain detachment. He can hob-nob on an equality with other leaders. It is, indeed, another instance of people tending to interact more with their equals than with their inferiors, or superiors.

As organizer, however, he is in a difficulty, and one we have already mentioned. There is an undercurrent of conflict between task activities and purely social intercourse, between efficiency and companionship, between control and the relaxed enjoyment of egalitarian friendship. This is all brought out in those elaborate analyses of Bales, when he depicts a discussion group as involving a field of tension between processes leading to the solution of a problem, and the disagreeable effects of being controlled by other people.

In the development of the prestige system, the group may give marks for good fellowship rather than for efficiency. This may obviously lead to inefficiency if the two do not go together. If they feel the task to be urgent, they are likely to give marks for efficiency, or what appears as such. Then, as we have seen, after a while popularity and leadership may become separated.

One may say that on the whole people do not like being ordered about, even, it would appear, having to submit to suggestions in a discussion which they admit to be good. The formal leader, too, is in the same difficulty; one is tempted to say that the more he leads the less he will be liked.

This is, however, too sweeping. A group may be attractive for several reasons. It may provide companionship, it may be the means of reaching ends which individual members desire, it may, through its reputation, endow its members with prestige in the outside world. In cases in which the group is a means towards an end, other than the provision of companionship, which the members want, the leader may give orders or initiate activities which are so clearly in accord with the achievement of the goals which the followers have at heart, that the satisfaction of approaching the goal outweighs the dissatisfaction of being controlled. On the other hand, the leader may give orders for action which does not appear to bring the followers closer to whatever goal lies before them at the moment, and even may remove them from it. The informal leader, as representative of the group, is less likely to be in this position; the formal leader is very frequently in it. It is, therefore, not so much being led that people resent, as being controlled by some external power whose intentions are not coincident with theirs.

From this it would appear to follow that in order to mitigate the almost inevitable resentment at being ordered about, some technique is required to align the interests of those who have to obey with those who give the orders. The aims of such technique are to explain the measures to be taken, so that they do not appear arbitrary, and to get agreement to their introduction, so that those who have to carry them out are already committed to co-operate.

Various techniques of this kind have been tried out in industry. Forms of joint ownership are intended to give the operatives a stake in the welfare of the business. Joint consultation is used as an occasion for explaining future developments and changes, and for persuading the operatives to agree to them. The difficulties which beset joint consultation have been frequently discussed. Apart from the mutual suspicion across the table, which even a supply of managerial cigarettes often fails to dissipate, there are two major difficulties to overcome. If joint consultation is to be a reality the committee cannot remain purely consultative; it must have power. If it is to have power, it must be able to commit the company to incur financial expenditure, and the workers to do what they are asked to do. Neither side is prepared to go to such extremes. Management hesitates to allow a joint consultative committee to decide on financial policy, and the representatives of the workers are liable to insist that they are only delegates when it comes to committing their fellows to do things they will not relish doing.

A third technique is what might be called 'joint committal', which is of particular interest because it introduces an extra factor in addition to mere agreement. This type of persuasion was first publicized by Lewin.[20] During World War II it was felt necessary to persuade housewives in America to serve offal to their husbands. To those who are only too glad to get hold of sweetbreads and kidneys, this will seem odd, but the fact remains that to the American housewife 'intestinals' were looked upon askance. Two techniques were used: attractive lectures on the nutritional value of such foods, and group discussions leading to a group decision. A follow-up survey showed that the latter method was overwhelmingly the more successful. The same thing was done to induce mothers to get their families to consume more milk and their babies to consume more orange juice.

These are, no doubt, humble beginnings for a principle of outstanding importance. The same technique was used by Bavelas[21] to increase the output of sewing machine operators. Another well-documented instance of its application is provided by Coch and French,[22] who compared the effects of what we have called joint-committal, group representation, and absence of any participation whatever, in a situation in which a change of procedure was introduced into an industrial process. Change of process is nearly always accompanied by a drop in production, due to frustration as well as to any difficulty there may be in learning a new technique. Here, again, joint-committal showed its merits.

All these investigations have been influenced by 'Field-Theory', and explain the advantages of this method of analysis. The individual member of a group is, as it were, held in position by the forces in the field which constitute a pressure upon him to conform. If you try to influence him individually, you are up against these powerful forces which drag him back to the level of activity established by the group. This level itself is determined by the forces tending towards increased production meeting the forces tending towards decrease of production.

What you have to do, in Lewin's terminology, is to 'unfreeze' the existing level by discussion, persuasion, and agreement, and then 'freeze' the new arrangement of forces at a higher level, or anyway at whatever level approximates to your intentions. A new conformity is established and, like the old one, carries the individual member with it. As Lewin puts it: 'it is easier to change the ideology and social practice of a small group handled together than of single individuals.' [23]

It is this principle that lies behind the successes of Alcoholics Anonymous, and has inspired the slogan of the Chicago Area Project, already mentioned, to the effect that if you want to tackle delinquency you must 'change the streets' in which the delinquents live. It is the same principle which is having such powerful effects in the People's Republic of China, to which reference will be made in the next chapter.

We may conclude this one by referring to another simple principle which operates throughout the whole range of group psychology. The cohesiveness of a group, by which we mean the motivating influences which keep its individual members in it, are a function of the forces in favour of membership and the forces against membership, in which are included external attractions. The forces in favour of membership are the rewards which membership brings together with the disrewards that membership enables one to avoid. The rewards of membership are internal and external. The internal rewards are such things as companionship, the achievement of goals which can only be reached through group activity and the prestige of belonging. The external rewards are such things as financial or other material gains. If, then, a group is to be kept together in situations of stress, where there is danger of its falling apart, either you must increase the internal rewards, or the external rewards, or the risks of non-membership, or all three.

This is obvious enough. The reason for dwelling on it is that it very often happens that people think of groups from their own, rather than from the members' point of view. They cannot understand, for instance, why young men prefer to stand in groups at street corners, rather than join the delightful clean-living club in the next street. They seldom pause to think that for them the internal rewards of a street corner gang are superior to those of club membership. If it were the other way about, the club would attract more members. The formulation of group behaviour in terms of forces, valences, vectors and so on has an air of bogus precision about it, but it does help us to rid ourselves of a great many foolish misunderstandings.

CHAPTER 10

CROWDS AND OTHER GROUPS

In Chapter 4 a distinction was made between the relatively permanent group in which a person may be said to live, such as a village or an urban neighbourhood, a special purpose group with some continuity, such as a factory unit, a school class, or a boy scouts' patrol, and a group brought together for special experimental purposes. The second type of group has been omitted, save in so far as examples form part of experimental material, because most of the work done on such groups has been done in the industrial field, and this is already covered in another volume of this series. The other two kinds of 'primary' or 'face-to-face' group have been discussed in the previous chapters.

There are, however, many kinds of groups which are not easily classified under these headings, groups of people under peculiar circumstances. In this chapter some of these will be considered.

The Crowd. In some of the earlier books on psychology, the only topic which had anything to do with social psychology was the psychology of the crowd, a topic which has received considerable attention. A crowd has been defined as 'a gathering of a considerable number of persons around a centre or point of common attention'.[1] This criterion of polarization distinguishes a 'crowd' in the psychological sense from a crowd in the sense of a mere aggregate of people in the same place at the same time, as in a 'crowded' street at the rush hour. The definition, however, groups together two types of groups of this ephemeral kind which it is convenient to keep apart: the crowd and the audience. It is perfectly true that audiences may display crowd phenomena of the kind we are about to consider, but there is a certain formality in their coming together, which we do not associate with crowds.

There is general agreement that a person who is a full member of a crowd, not a mere spectator watching from the periphery, is liable to behave differently from the way he would behave if he were by himself. This is so striking that some authors, such as Le Bon, one of the best known writers on the subject, feel inclined to postulate some kind of 'collective mind'. Such a hypothesis, suggested no doubt by the homogeneity of the crowd, is unnecessary; the behaviour of its members can be accounted for in a simple way.

The first notable feature is a heightening of emotionality. The man in the presence of danger feels frightened; in the presence of other people experiencing and evincing the same emotion his fear is enhanced. This may be due to some inherent tendency to reflect in oneself the emotion displayed by others: what Mac-Dougall called 'primative sympathy'. This, however, is not a very satisfactory hypothesis, because we are by no means always induced automatically to feel the same emotion as is displayed by someone else. In the case of fear the conception of the danger itself is magnified when we observe other people terrified, and this works cumulatively because everyone observes everyone else. Where, as in the case of a fire in a theatre, a stampede for the exit may well prejudice the chances of people behind reaching safety, the enhancement of fear is perfectly realistic. Another and slightly different cause of the enhancement of emotion will appear later on.

Another feature is the lowering of a sense of responsibility, a diminution of our powers of criticism, and a slackening of normal controls. This has been put down to the 'impression of universality', the notion that so many other people can't be wrong. We have, as Miller and Dollard[2] point out, been rewarded when we have acted as other people act, and penalized for non-conformity. Thus we have learnt to accept the leadership of others. This, however, is only likely to have a massive effect if the emotions and behaviour displayed by the others find an echo in ourselves. We believe there is danger, this is confirmed by the fear displayed by other people, the danger must be terrific, they rush for the door, we rush with redoubled vigour.

In the case of aggressive or destructive crowds, however, another factor seems to come in. People in the crowd are not only more excited, they are liable to behave in a way they themselves

F   161

would consider reprehensible. The crowd-situation seems to allow a release to motives which are otherwise controlled, even if conscious, or to motives of which the actor may be unaware. Not only that, they may do the most violent things with a 'good' conscience. In psycho-analytic terminology, the crowd, with its prestige of numbers, takes the place of their 'super-egos'. Where a leader emerges this is even more clearly the case; the followers, in Freud's words, seem to have 'substituted one and the same object for their Ego Ideal and have consequently identified themselves with one another in their ego'.[3]

A great many social psychologists have given crowds a bad name. Le Bon admitted that they were capable of heroism and self-sacrifice, but he was, on political grounds, against them; 'Isolated,' he says, 'a man may be a cultured individual; in a crowd he is a barbarian.' This, however, is not the case. In a crowd, stirred with emotions of compassion, the individual's cautionary controls may be swept away, just as much as his controls over his hostility; he does not wish to be outdone.

What happens may very well depend on the leadership the crowd happens to receive and to accept. In conditions of danger which might provoke a panic reaction, the right kind of leadership may lead to acts of heroism. What is the 'right kind of leadership' doubtless depends on the crowd itself. Sighele,[4] for instance, contrasts two strikes. In 1886 the miners of Decazeville murdered their chief engineer. In a strike in Rome a crowd of workmen all agog to act destructively were prevented from doing so by a single man. In the first case the ringleader was a man with a criminal record, in the second the members of the crowd had unblemished records. Our decent impulses are just as much part of us as our less decent ones. Either of them may be fortified – if they are both present.

In a crowd, then, you have a number of people united together by the experiencing of the same emotion and the same call to action. What mechanism will be called into play will vary from situation to situation: sometimes fear is intensified, sometimes unconscious aggression is allowed expression, sometimes generosity is allowed free range, sometimes heroism defeats the instinct of self-preservation. In all cases there is an intensification of whatever motives find expression.

So far, so good, but people do not always panic in the face of danger and people do not always set out to destroy the objects of their detestation. We must look further for the causes of crowd formation. We look in two directions: individual differences and the general social climate.

In a series of observations of children, Grosser, Polansky and Lippitt[5] found that individuals with high prestige were imitated in situations in which the activities in question were officially acceptable, but that when it came to kicking over the traces 'impulsive' children gave the lead. May it not be that a crowd is 'triggered off' by people whose 'thresholds of mob-involvement', as Roger W. Brown[6] rather inelegantly puts it, are low?

Lynchings are typical examples of aggressive crowd action. Colonel Charles Lynch, who provided a name for unofficial methods of dealing with crime, seems to have been a Revolutionary patriot who organized leading citizens in Virginia to take steps against those who were injuring their cause. Apparently his unofficial courts were run on judicial principles, they did not exact the death penalty, and they merely filled a gap left by the inadequacies of the official courts.[7] Since then the name has acquired a darker colour.

It seems, however, that we must distinguish between what Cantril[8] and others have called 'Bourbon' and 'proletariat' lynchings. The former consists of action taken by leading citizens to deal with some specific crime. Other Negroes are protected, and the mob is alleged to be small and orderly. This is more like the activities of the original Lynch. The 'proletariat' lynching is action by a mob, and usually occurs where the Negroes are in a minority and where the object is persecution. In the latter cases it appears that the ringleaders are lawless persons, frequently with police records. The suggestion is that in aggressive crowd action it is triggered off by the impulsive or by those whose controls have already worn rather thin, that they create a kind of permissive atmosphere which attracts the waverers, who, in turn, are watched by passive supporters.

Such an explanation may well hold for aggressive crowds, but does not necessarily hold for other examples of crowd activity. It is the assumption that crowd action is always violent that has led a good deal of 'crowd-psychology' astray.

Panic, for example, is the direct response to danger; there is no need to suppose that there is any criminal element involved at all. The cases which spring to mind are cases in which there is no previous drill to enable people to face danger with courage. It sometimes, however, occurs in groups, such as military units. This frequently occurs when leadership fails, and many writers believe this to be the main factor in the situation. If, as the Freudians hold, the leader holds the group together, when he disappears the group flies apart unless someone quickly takes his place. When organization breaks down, *sauve qui peut*.

Danger may suddenly present itself without warning, and without our having to go further than the episode itself to account for panic. Some crowd action, however, riots, strikes, and revolutionary crowd manifestations require for their occurrence a past history of tension. This general atmosphere may be called upon to explain panic as well in certain circumstances. On 30 October 1938 there was a realistic broadcast in America of an invasion from Mars which produced an extraordinary effect. 'Long before the broadcast had ended,' says Cantril, who analysed the episode, 'people all over the United States were praying, crying, fleeing frantically to escape death from the Martians. Some ran to rescue loved ones. Others telephoned farewells or warnings, hurried to inform neighbours, sought information from newspapers or radio-stations, summoned ambulances and police cars.'[9] This is not, strictly speaking, the reaction of a *crowd*, because they were not all in the same place at the same time, but it is crowd-like conduct. Why was the broadcast believed? For the majority of listeners, no doubt, it remained within the frame of reference of a broadcast, for those who were taken in it was a situation for which there was no ready response whatever. Now Cantril suggests that this readiness to take it seriously was in part due to prolonged economic unrest and depression. This rendered people insecure and lowered their critical sense.

It is almost certain that some past history is required to account for what the Americans call 'wild-cat' strikes. An eye-witness account of a strike at a Scottish pit brings this out.[10] The strippers were waiting to go down the pit for the afternoon shift, they sat about in the sun in the groups in which they worked. Among them were strippers who had been moved from another pit where they got 35s. instead of 30s. a shift, and were naturally disgruntled. At 1.20 the men of one of the sections said that it was too fine to go to work. At 1.30 they got up and taunted the others for being such suckers as to go to work on such a nice afternoon. Some of the members of the other groups joined the ones who were standing together and the word went round that 'strippers of section B are on strike'. By 1.40 they had all joined, keeping to their sections, and within the sections pairs of men would start talking violently to one another, forming a focus of attention for the men of their group, and complaining about conditions of work. At 1.50 one of the crowd demanded that they should stand out for 35s. a shift.

The crowd was now unified. At 2.10 the colliery agent and the manager came to persuade them to go down, offering to receive a deputation next morning. This was unsuccessful. One man got on a wall and urged them to agree. Another pointed out that if those who were ready to go down did so, those who were not yet changed would be victimized. This won the day and it was agreed to have a union meeting that evening. This decision was a relief and they all went home. The 'diffused "againstness"', as the writer of this account put it, had been focused on to a purpose; they had found an appropriate leader and the aggressiveness faded. This simple episode illustrates the chance happening which touches off an explosive situation. In this particular case the explosive charge was relatively small, and the men returned to work next day.

This strike had a definite wage dispute behind it. In the wild-cat strike at 'Oscar Centre', described by Alvin W. Gouldner,[11] the strike was precipitated by a shop steward calling a production specialist a 'yellow bastard'. In two hours the strike was on. The two-hour interval really removes this case from crowd-psychological theory, but the case itself, as analysed by Gouldner, has significant points.

According to Scott and Homans,[12] who studied wild-cat strikes in Detroit, the strikes were seldom concerned with wages; they were rather concerned with informal grievances. Now in Oscar Centre, a gypsum company, there had been a tradition of informal leniency. Clocking in was slack, taking material home for household purposes was tacitly allowed, foremen were accepted in the primary groups of workmen, the code was that the workmen were there to work and did not need close supervision. These informal arrangements correspond to Homans' 'Internal System'. For various reasons management thought it necessary to tighten things up. The workers had no *legitimate* complaint. It is true that they did divert their hostility at one point into a wage issue, but when their demands were granted, they still felt indignant.

Close supervision in connexion with new machinery was forced on them, men who had had long service with the company were demoted, and the union officials were dilatory. Tension mounted, as it does in all groups, because mutual expectations were frustrated. The very fact that these expectations were non-contractual and therefore could not go through the normal channels led to their mounting up and exploding at the sound of a swear word.

Here we have the usual background of smouldering animosity which is a prerequisite for so much crowd action, but in this case the important principle comes out quite clearly that unofficial tensions, that is to say tensions of which there is no official cognizance, are often more explosive than disputes which can come out into the open.

The Audience. Obviously audiences vary according to the occasion of their meeting. Kimball Young[13] suggests a classification: information-seeking, recreation-seeking, and conversional. This order is obviously the order in which crowd-like phenomena are likely to appear. The lecture hall is scarcely the place for the display of emotion. The theatre, on the other hand, goes to some pains to polarize the audience by the introductory music, the lightened stage and the darkened auditorium. The feel of '*rapport*' between the members of the audience and the actors, and between themselves is more likely to develop, though we are told[14] that in an American University town, Wednesday is not a good night for the theatre because it was an evening on which the boys took their girls out, and thus had their attention divided – if that.

The 'conversional' audience, on the other hand, is called together for the purpose, not of instruction, not of entertainment, but of persuasion. Here every device may be used to generate a homogeneous and submissive attitude in the assembly. The bands may play, processions may focus attention, the speaker is raised up and spotlighted, and the audience may be drawn together by community singing. Something akin to the strange phenomena of hypnotism seems to be at work, and recipes for inducing a receptive attitude have been set forth by many writers, including Hitler in *Mein Kampf*.

In its uncritical frame of mind the audience is presented with emotive language, and highly coloured imagery. 'Imagine yourselves', cried Jonathan Edwards,[15] 'to be cast into a fiery oven or a great furnace, where your pain would be as much greater than that occasioned by accidentally touching a coal of fire as the heat is greater. Imagine also that your body were to lie there for a quarter of an hour, full of fire and all the time full of quick sense. . . . How long would that quarter of an hour seem to you? . . . But what would be the effect upon your soul if you must lie there enduring that torment for twenty-four hours? . . . a whole year . . . a thousand years. Oh! then how would your heart sink if you knew that you must bear it for ever and ever – that there would be no end, that for millions and millions of ages, your torments would be no nearer to an end and that you never, never would be delivered. But your torment in hell will be immensely greater than this illustration represents.'

No wonder strange effects have been reported, as, for example, from a revival meeting in Kentucky in 1801:[16] 'At no time was the floor less than half covered. Some lay quiet unable to move or speak. Some talked but could not move. Some beat the floor with their heels. Some, shrieking in agony, bounded about like live fish out of water. Some lay down and rolled over and over for hours at a time. Others rushed wildly over the stumps and benches and then plunged, shouting "Lost! Lost!" into the forest.'

The response to the speaker repeating: 'Come. Come. Come now. Come. Come now . . .' is scarcely surprising in the light of the Kentucky revival.

Like all crowd phenomena such abandonment must be ascribed to a multiplicity of causes, personal and social. According to the type of meeting, whether religious or political, various motivations, conscious and unconscious, are appealed to in the individuals present. It may be aggression, it may be guilt, it may be sex, it may be a need for security and leadership – motivation and needs idiosyncratic to individuals. But the social climate and even fashion have to be brought into the picture. Whatever the personal problem of individuals may be, they may all share a sense of oppression, a sense of insecurity and a 'diffuse "against-ness"'. There may, too, be a vogue of crowd behaviour, like the dancing mania of the Middle Ages.

In addition to this, even broader traditions have to be considered. In a society in which it is considered bad form to display emotion, there will be less likelihood of emotional excess, because everyone is drilled to contain himself. Where, however, this is not the case, what we think of as 'crowd phenomena' may be more easily elicited. An English crowd, for example, is never likely to behave like an Indian one.

Groups under stress. In the previous chapters we have been dealing either with people living normal lives in groups or with subjects taking part in laboratory experiments. The latter are, admittedly, in a somewhat unusual situation, but it is not exactly one of threatening danger or oppression.

We will now consider one or two situations, studied by social psychologists, in which groups are under unusual and stressful pressure.

The views of W. R. Bion. The first study may be regarded as misplaced. The subjects studied by Dr Bion at the Tavistock Clinic were sometimes patients and sometimes not, but they exhibited certain features of group life that do not normally obtrude. They were, to a certain extent, placed in a disturbing situation by Dr Bion himself, as will be seen in what follows. The account is based on seven articles published in *Human Relations*.[17]

His groups consisted of eight or nine people, sometimes more, sometimes less. They met ostensibly, so it would appear, either to study a group in action, or for therapeutic purposes. We are not concerned with the therapeutic aspect as such, but with the nature of the groups as they presented themselves to Dr Bion's sensitive perception. Meeting as they did for a purpose, they expected a definite form, an order of procedure, a lecture, a seminar, or a therapeutic session of their own imagining. This they did not get from Dr Bion. He tried to refrain from accepting any of the roles they implied by their behaviour. In fact, as he almost confesses, he behaved extremely oddly, and even badly, from the group's point of view. The result of this was that the groups, left in a sense to their own devices, frequently showing hostility to and rejection of the psychiatrist who clearly was not doing his job, displayed by their behaviour the underlying springs of action of which they were unaware, and which, indeed they wanted to avoid.

What, then, were these undercurrents? Dr Bion describes episodes that occurred and the various interpretations he gave of them: he describes, too, the way in which he developed and altered his explanatory framework. We can only consider here his final conclusions. To begin with he noted that every member of the group was constantly forming an estimate of the attitude of the group towards himself. Secondly he found that the group had a kind of self-preservative instinct. If members were absent, discomfort was felt, partly, no doubt, because the absentees showed their contempt for the group, and thereby made its members wonder whether they were not being fools for attending themselves, but partly because their absence displayed a breach in the group itself. Conversation would centre round the absentees, and, indeed, on one occasion Dr Bion goes so far as to say that the group seemed to be led by them in their very absence.

This solidarity gradually assumed in Dr Bion's mind, as he sensed its operation, a more definite shape – indeed, several shapes. It is at this point that his observations gave rise to his theory. He frequently insists that the reality can only be conveyed in a somewhat feeble way by description, and we have to rely on his personal conviction, which can, of course, be verified by others with the same sensibilities. In the tangle of conversation, sometimes emotional, sometimes trivial, sometimes carried on in pairs, sometimes leading to embarrassed silences, he detected a kind of unconscious collusion. It seemed as though he was confronted by individuals with conscious motives, and some whole in which they were participating. He finds himself forced to speak of a 'group mentality'.

From the emotions expressed, from the way in which his own interpretations of what was going on were received, and from the situations, such, for example, as expressed hostility, which seemed to give satisfaction to the more aggressive members, he got the impression that the 'group mentality' operated with three 'basic assumptions'. There was the 'pairing' assumption, which was manifested when the group split into pairs, and which assumed a sexual basis for such activities; secondly there was the 'fight or flight' assumption, the assumption that the group had met to attack an enemy or to defend itself against a danger; thirdly there is the 'basic assumption' 'that the group has met together to obtain security from one individual on whom they depend'.

'Group mentality is the unanimous expression of the will of the group, contributed to by the individual in ways of which he is unaware, influencing him disagreeably whenever he thinks or behaves at variance with its basic assumption.' Here we have the source of conflict and embarrassment. The individual members of a group are in varying degrees sophisticated; they are there for a purpose. They form, indeed, what Bion calls a 'work group', with conscious intention to co-operate in an enterprise: the scientific study of groups, the cure of neurosis, or some other purpose. The individual is thus torn in twain. If he fits in with the 'basic assumption' of the group, he feels that his purposes are being unfulfilled, or he hates the scientific terms with which he has to operate; if he concentrates on the working aspect, he feels the undertow of the group.

We do not learn much about the phases in which 'pairing' or 'fight and flight' are dominant as 'basic assumptions' but we do get valuable information about 'depending'. Here the assumption is that the group can get security from someone in whom they can place implicit trust. The therapist, in Bion's groups, is the obvious choice, but the need for security is, as it were, an all or none affair, it is the need for magical security. Dr Bion's scientific explanations, and explicit denial of the role of magician, did not go down at all well. This, surely, is familiar outside the therapeutic field. Are there not many groups of believers who bitterly resent discussion of their tenets in scientific terms? They are not confined by any means to what would ordinarily be called 'religious' groups. There are groups who prate of Science and detest it when they meet it face to face.

When the assumption of depending dominates, then, the group seeks a magical source of security. Here, as we have done above, Bion himself passes beyond the confines of his own groups into the wider field of group psychology. The kind of protection such groups seek is best satisfied by a supra-human being, or, at second best, by the spirit of a dead authority. The living human is disturbing. If he is found and fills the position, that may satisfy one need, but it threatens another. There is a fear of dictatorship. Groups in this particular frame of mind will therefore always demand a return to a belief in God, following St Augustine whose *The City of God* is the satisfying dream of the 'basic assumption of depending'. Groups operating with other 'basic assumptions' will look elsewhere.

One curious feature of therapeutic groups in the dependence phase is that when the therapist fails them it chooses one of its members as leader, and almost always 'its most ill member'. The mad have often been deemed holy, and anything is better than rationality.

It must be admitted, as Dr Bion points out, that in a group of patients there is the tendency to 'act on basic assumptions basically', and he further insists on the vitality of the conscious 'work group', saying that it 'triumphs in the long run'. The study of the group of patients is valuable because they manifest more excessively group suasions to which we are all responsive in virtue of our being social animals. The peculiar value of Bion's research lies in his emphasis on the unconscious group influences which are at work, not only in therapeutic groups, but in other groups as well. The suggestion is that the nature of the devices we use to keep the group together, the evasion of difficulties, the indignation and disappointment we sometimes feel are due, in part at least, to the conflict between our conscious aims and the unconscious influences of the groups to which we belong.

The Army. The manifest function of an army is to fight, whether it be against the army of another country, or against a rebel force. It may incidentally serve as a character-building institution, broadening the minds and the experience of its members, but the training they receive must be calculated to inculcate habits of discipline and disregard of danger.

One of the methods used to this end is to group soldiers in units in which they are expected to become, as the Americans put it, 'ego-involved'. The authorities are aided in this by the desire of the soldier himself to have something which, in his eyes and in the eyes of his companions, is worth identifying himself with, a group which gives him distinction and prestige. This is achieved by laying stress on regimental history and repute, by distinctive marks of membership, by the growth of regimental mythology and customs, and, in some cases, by linking army units with different parts of the country. The general aim is to induce loyalty so that as well as habits of obedience learnt in training there is an additional control established which prevents the soldier doing anything that 'lets the regiment down'.

The actual unit with which soldiers identify themselves is probably the regiment. Without further research it is difficult to be certain, but where one is dealing with the rank and file it is doubtful whether such remote groups as 'Army' and 'Country' are very significant beyond verbal acquiescence in the demand to do well by the one and to love the other.

Such, at any rate, seems to have been the case in the American Army according to Professor Shils.[18] He has gone through the massive volumes of *The American Soldier*, a compendium of information about the conduct of the United States Army in the last war, to find out how important primary groups seem to have been. In the view of the compilers of this study: 'The primary group served two principal functions in combat motivation: it set and emphasized group standards of behaviour and it supported and sustained the individual in stresses he would otherwise not have been able to withstand.' These are related functions: the group enforced its standards principally by offering or withholding recognition, respect, and approval, which were among the supports it had to offer, while the subjective reward of following the internalized group code enhanced the individual's resources for dealing with the situation.[19]

An American soldier, Bill Mauldin, writes: 'During the three years I spent in the 45th Division I was certain that it was not only the best division in the Army, but that it *was* the Army.'[20] Two psychologists, Grinker and Spiegel, writing of the Air Force, say: 'The men and their plane become identified with each other with an intensity that in civil life is found only within the family circle.'[21]

The group provides a sense of power and security, and it was found that infantrymen who came overseas with their units were less subject to fear than were replacements. The latter had to take on the ethos of the group of veterans to which they were assigned, but 'the larger the population of new-comers the greater the resistance of the primary group to their assimilation', though the rate of assimilation was increased by combat. It was also found among the German troops that Army units with a high degree of primary group integrity suffered little from deserters or from individually contrived surrender.[22] The unity here was often impeded by language difficulties when Czechs, Poles, and other nationals were drafted into German units, and in the latter days of the war primary groups were often broken up, thereby making surrender more likely.

The importance of the primary group can be expressed by saying that the group acts as the 'super-ego' of its members. This is in line with the concept of the officer as exemplar, particularly in combat. In non-combat areas his function is more that of protector. In the German Army, when experienced officers and N.C.O.s were in short supply, their inexperienced successors often failed in their function because they did not know the names of their men. It is interesting to note that in the American Army the officers were more trusted than the N.C.O.s. They have to be somewhat remote, somewhat mysterious, and endowed with a slightly magic power by their followers. We are reminded of Bion's groups with the basic assumption of dependence uppermost. The N.C.O.s are the immediate source of deprivation, and that naturally arouses hostility.

Shils' study of the importance of primary groups in the American and the German Armies is largely applicable to our own. The importance of the primary group has been stressed throughout this book. A caveat, however, must be entered here. While the primary group is of paramount importance as a controlling agency, the norms which it enforces, and its relation to the superior ranks in charge of it, will vary from culture to culture. The norms of the primary group in the Japanese Army will be different from those in the British Army. The relation between officers and men must necessarily vary with the cultural arrangement of its prestige system. The relations will be different in a culture in which inequality is deprecated from what they are where inequality is accepted as right and proper. One instance of a possible difference in norms is mentioned by Shils. He says that toughness, masculinity, and aggression are cultivated by the American soldier, and he ascribes this to a reaction against latent homosexuality. One doubts whether this particular emphasis is to be found in all armies.

Another contrast can be drawn between the American and British Armies and the German Army: the former always wanted to know how their actions fitted in with a general plan of campaign, the latter were not bothered about such matters. The demand for explanations and the frequent experience of getting them fit in with our general climate of opinion; the unquestioning acceptance of orders fits in with other features of German culture. As we have frequently said, the primary group is never to be treated in isolation. It is always influenced by the wider culture to which its members belong.

Prisoners of War. The hardships and dangers to which the armed forces may be subjected are serious enough in all conscience, but those who face them are at least playing active roles, and roles approved of by themselves, by their comrades, and indeed by the world at large. They are the reverse of ignominious.

The prisoner of war, on the other hand, is in a very different position. However unjustified he may be, he is likely to feel guilty at being captured and guilty because he is removed from the scene of combat. He now has no role, he has nothing particular to do, he is thrown back on his own resources, he has to safeguard his personality, and he is, or may be, never alone.

In civilian life a man has a variety of roles with which he can identify himself, in which he plays a part, well or ill, which is accepted by society. He knows what is expected of him; he has a defined place. In the Army, this is also the case, though the system of expectations is different, and it is often difficult for him to go back to the systems of civilian life when he is demobilized. In the prisoner of war camp there are no known positions with appropriate roles to play. He is, one might say, stripped of his social clothing, and faces his fellow prisoners naked.

In a book called *Barbed Wire Disease*,[23] an expression coined for a syndrome of symptoms found in prisoners of war in World War I, Dr A. L. Vischer of Basel produces evidence from his own experience of the plight of prisoners. His cases are mainly French and German. The main complaint voiced is the lack of privacy. The prisoners have to be adjusting themselves to other people all the time. Of course everyone reacts differently, but they all have the same problem: to preserve their identity. 'Many of the prisoners', he says, 'combine fault-finding with a passion for declaring themselves superior to their neighbours; they snobbishly boast of their social position and high connections and make themselves out to be persons of importance.' This sensitivity in social intercourse gives rise to extreme irritability 'so that they cannot stand the slightest opposition and readily fly into a passion. A mania for discussion develops, but sound judgement is entirely lacking in the argument.' This irritability among people who are thrown into constant contact with one another has, of course, been frequently reported from other sources, but in the prisoner of war it is combined with a lack of anything to do which seems worth doing. The result, according to Dr Vischer, is apathy, extreme restlessness, inability to concentrate, and loss of memory.

In spite of these uneasy relationships, the camp achieves a

certain unity, 'a collective individuality, with its own peculiarities and disposition'. This, no doubt, may tend to intensify the individual symptoms; it certainly provides a field for rumour to develop and a climate constantly changing from exaggerated hope to despair.

Again, we note cultural differences. Dr Kinnier Wilson, who introduces Dr Vischer's book, quotes an English prisoner of war as saying that the Russians in his experience were 'a cheerful lot, considering everything, little given to thinking of their situation'. It is likely that people who are used to very little privacy would not resent its absence to the same extent that would be the case with people who made a cult of it.

The English prisoner of war in World War II has received a good deal of attention from the social psychologist. Professor Curle,[24] who worked with the Civilian Resettlement Units, set up to assist prisoners of war who found difficulty in re-establishing themselves, describes how, after an initial phase of psychological disturbance, some kind of social life emerged. It was 'an impoverished culture', but one in which 'men ultimately took up once more the role of a soldier, but this time without weapons; they developed a cultural war with the enemy which not only diminished the painful loss of self-respect and the burden of guilt and inferiority but at the same time offered an outlet for the hostility and bitterness arising from their frustrated and timeless experience'. They were sustained by the knowledge that international organizations were protecting them, and, in the case of the Red Cross, materially assisting them. They had found, in some sense, a collective purpose.

Their experience, however, made it far more difficult to settle down to civilian life when they were released. The civilian role system was too different from the one to which they had adapted themselves. It was to help them that therapeutic units were set up, to act as a kind of bridge between life in a prison camp, life back in the army, and life in 'civvy street'. In setting up these units an attempt was made to make use of the positive gains of prisoner of war life. This may seem strange, but the prisoners had devised some kind of democratic 'way of life', and in some ways they were more mature than their fellows. The trouble was that they were plunged into an entirely different system of expectations. The function of the Civilian Resettlement Units was to use their capacities for discussion and getting on together under difficult conditions to help them bit by bit to cope with new and unexpected difficulties. The results of the enterprise show the enormous value of the transitional experience.

Concentration Camps. According to Dr Vischer the symptoms he detected among his prisoners of war were not affected by goodness or badness of treatment. True, there was undermining of resistance through lack of food, but there was no suggestion of positive cruelty.

What, then, happens when, in addition to the lack of privacy, the pointlessness of existence and the shame of imprisonment, you have the additional horror of diabolical cruelty?

We are fortunate in having an account of such a situation from the pen of a psychologist who was imprisoned in Dachau and Buchenwald between 1938 and 1939.[25] The author himself, Dr Bettelheim, was determined to preserve his personality intact, and he found this possible because of his professional training and interests. Certain features of his account are already familiar. The need for self-support made the politically educated prisoners feel important because their very plight demonstrated how important they were. The upper-class prisoners also took refuge in their importance and 'looked down on all other prisoners nearly as much as they despised the Gestapo'. As time and misery and horror went on certain changes occurred, mostly among the non-political prisoners, who had in their lives outside the camp partly accepted the Nazi régime. First the less extreme cruelties were dealt with as they would be dealt with in ordinary life. Slaps and minor indignities aroused indignation, but serious assaults, which were so extreme as to be unthinkable, were unresented, save for a general rage against the system. Day-dreams developed and were communicated as realities, supporting the importance of the dreamer. And then came the final submission, which 'would not have taken place if it had not happened in all prisoners', except the few who managed to preserve some precarious kind of detachment, like Dr Bettelheim. They became like children.

'Prisoners would, like adolescents, fight one another tooth and nail, only to become close friends within a few minutes.' And, like children, they gradually accepted the standards of their superiors.

'A prisoner had reached the final stage of adjustment to the camp situation when he changed his personality so as to accept the values of the Gestapo.' They copied their terms of abuse, they copied their games, and they tried, with their miserable resources and such bits as they could steal, to dress like their captors. 'When asked why they did it they admitted that they loved to look like one of the guards.'

This surely displays the power of social prestige. To begin with the Gestapo conduct was odious and contemptible. Their victims then became inured to a new life. They are back again as children, ill-treated perhaps, but now that they have lost touch with the outer world for ever, this is a new life and as children they take on the standards of their ruthless 'fathers'. This, according to Dr Bettelheim, is exactly what was intended.

Civil Prisons. The last example of groups of men under stress is the civil prison community. Here the stress is very different from what it is in the other two types of imprisonment. The deprivations are different from those in the prisoner of war camps and not so severe as those in concentration camps. The prisoners are in public disgrace, though their own attitudes will vary from individual to individual according to the crimes he has committed. Some doubtless feel guilty, for some it is just in the luck of the game, while others – homosexual offenders, for example – feel that their 'crime' is no crime at all. Nevertheless, in so far as they associate with one another they form a primary group.

It is not easy to get accurate information about the nature of such groups. Details of the formal system, what Homans might call the external system, are available to anyone who chooses to look up the right books. It is the informal or internal system that is hard to gauge. Books are occasionally written by ex-prisoners, but they are usually concerned with expressing complaints against the 'system' – bad food, bad drainage, inadequate library facilities, and so on. They do, however, depict a society with its friendships, its jealousies, its status hierarchy, its 'tobacco barons', and, frequently, its good nature.

In America, Hans Riemer had the courage to be sent to prison for four months in order to study the prison community. This is, indeed, a handsome instance of 'participant observation'. He found that in his experience 'the prison population is largely in control of a small group of men which has two divisions. There are the "politicians" . . . who hold key positions in the administrative offices of the prison'. They can dispense benefits and are frequently 'racketeers'. On the whole they are disliked. 'The other section of the controlling powers is held by the "right guys". These men are so called because of the consistency of their behaviour in accordance with the criminal or prison code.'[26] In accordance with the views of Homans, the leaders are those who act up to the norms of the group. The code has two main principles: loyalty to other prisoners and hostility to prison officials.

Any new-comer must accept the code or he will be ostracized by his companions. While it has been estimated, for American prisons, that 'about forty per cent of prisoners are not in any way intimately integrated groups and that another forty per cent engage in some of the superficial practices of group life but are not genuinely affiliated with primary groups',[27] the code and its guardians must have some effect on everyone. The prestige system of any society is bound to influence all who are members of it. 'The prison dogma', write Sutherland and Cressey, 'serves, like the prison code, to demonstrate to the prisoners that they are different from, and in many ways superior to, their own criminal keepers.' This may be far more harmful than any tips the individual prisoner may get about ways of cracking open a safe.

None of this is at all surprising. After all, the criminal has his position in society to keep up. Society has condemned him. He must therefore find some other backing. The experienced prison inmate finds that there is nothing absolutely intolerable about prison life. He feels no guilt. Everyone knows what everyone else has done, and no one has cause to look down their noses. Prison life is a kind of life, it's no use moaning, let's make the best of it. The inexperienced prisoner, feeling, may be, ashamed and unnerved, is thankful to find himself among people who have been through what he has been through, have survived, look well, are prepared to accept him, and turn out, many of them, quite charming. He naturally wants to be liked and well thought of, and he therefore accepts the ethos of his new group.

This is, perhaps, a somewhat highly coloured picture. Some prisoners are doubtless conscience-stricken, many dislike the deprivations so much that they are deterred from doing anything that might bring them back again, but we have to remember that when a man is sent to prison he is made a member of a community which takes crime lightly and which is calculated to reinforce any anti-social attitude the novice may have.

Attempts have been made to change the situation by introducing a measure of self-government. This was tried in America as far back as 1793. There are difficulties, however. The 'politicians' and 'racketeers' often get into key positions and rule the roost to the disadvantage of their fellows, so much so that in the New Jersey State Reformatory the project was abandoned 'by a vote that was practically unanimous'.

Another device has been the use of group therapy, in the hope that the anti-criminal tendencies in the participants will be encouraged by the group. This may possibly be effective for the younger and less experienced prisoner, but one cannot feel much confidence in its efficacy for the more hardened 'patient'.

Yet another line of action is to modify the prison situation itself, by having so-called 'open prisons', such as the one at Sudbury in Derbyshire, where there are no bars, and where a more normal life can be lived. Such institutions, again, are only suitable for certain types of prisoner.

For the obstreperous young, experiments have been conducted by Aichhorn[28] and Wills[29] in the technique of *laissez-faire*. The violent were allowed to be violent until they discovered for themselves the discomforts of destruction.

In the civil prisons of China, where attempts are made to turn prisons into a collection of small factories, re-education is supposed to take place through work, discussion, and mutual criticism.

It is important that such experiments in group therapy, self-government, contact with the outer world, interesting employment, and even discussion, which is a form of therapy, should be carried out. It may be that only the young and those not deeply involved in crime will be influenced, but this in itself is obviously of the greatest value. In any case, our present techniques would seem to be powerless to alter the ethos of the standard prison society, if we can speak of such a thing. Such a community perpetuates the status and role of the criminal in society at large. Humanitarianism may bid us rejoice that they are not too depraved. Prudence bids us hope that, as time goes on, fewer and fewer will be contaminated.

CHAPTER 11

APPLICATIONS

In Chapters 7, 8, and 9 a very general survey has been given of recent research into what is known as 'group dynamics'. This kind of research and experimentation is perhaps of greater significance to the academic psychologist than to the layman. It is absurd to suggest that the scientist is interested in the detached observation of any phenomena he happens to come across, to imply, that is to say, that he is completely unselective, in his choice of objects to study. He is, of course, interested in certain general fields of inquiry; and he has theories and hunches which he wants to try out and which guide his research. At the same time it may be admitted that if one reviews the whole field of research into group activity one gets the impression of a somewhat disorderly agglomeration of investigation. This is because different social psychologists approach the subject from different points of view. Furthermore, the person who is not professionally concerned with the matter may be forgiven if he sometimes feels that social psychologists display enormous ingenuity in showing once and for all that the obvious is really as obvious as it seems.

All this has been already mentioned in Chapter 3 where a warning was issued to the effect that very little, if any, new information comes out of this experimental work. It is carried out in the interests of isolating variables, discovering simple rules, in the hope that systematization will eventually be possible. Oddly enough, the very familiarity of the material often makes its disentanglement more difficult.

The specialist, then, has his own preoccupation with systems, variables, rules, and methods of experimentation. For the general public they provide new emphasis, a kind of spotlighting of certain aspects of what they know already, and a bringing to self-consciousness of what is usually taken for granted.

To speak, then, of the 'application' of the principles, new orientations, and theoretical approaches that have been developed by the social psychologists in their study of small groups, to the problems of everyday life is to use the word in a slightly different sense from that in which it is used when we speak of the 'application' of the principle of nuclear fission to industry and transport. There one has a source of energy, which was hitherto unavailable, now made available, and you can think up ways in which it can be applied to turn the wheels of factories and motor cars. Again, a new drug is discovered, which has certain effects on the human mind. You think of situations in which these effects will be beneficial. Nothing like this occurs when the principles of group dynamics are 'applied'. Here one is in the main suggesting that we can get better results if we apply consciously and skilfully the principles we have already through the ages applied unconsciously and without realizing what we were up to.

It is true that some social psychologists will say that new engines – the engines engendered by group action – are now made available. But they were available before. The 'team spirit' may conceivably have been operative when the foundations of the Tower of Babel were laid; certainly the later stages of its construction displayed the significance of adequate lines of communication.

Besides this, even if we can argue that the systematic study of groups makes us realize things we did not appreciate before, this meagre amount of novelty is the less novel for another reason. It is argued by Marxists that new developments in science are symptoms of social change. New economic opportunities present themselves and the scientist explores the appropriate fields. This is no place to discuss this hypothesis.[1] There is obviously much to be said for it, though doubtless much scientific research cannot be directly linked up with contemporary economic requirements; science, once started, gains a momentum of its own. The element of truth in the hypothesis derives from the fact that scientific inquiry is not something that is carried out apart from the rest of society; it is part of the social process. On general grounds we would think that this must be particularly true of psychology, whether personal psychology or social psychology, because the subject-matter of the psychologist confronts him both in his laboratory and in everyday life in a way that is not the case with the subject-matter of the physicist or the chemist. The psychologist, unless he concentrates on the problem of perception or on learning-theory, is bound to be influenced by the changing estimations and evaluations of human personality and human interaction which social change brings about.

Thus it is plausible to suggest that the present preoccupation with group dynamics is a symptom of our times to a greater extent than is the case with any topic which holds the centre of the stage in any other science. It is arguable that the study of the individual personality in isolation from his social environment was appropriate to competitive capitalism, and that the new emphasis on social interaction is appropriate to a society which has become increasingly aware of itself as an interactive system.

There is, indeed, more in it than that. As was mentioned in Chapter 4 it is now being said on all sides that large-scale industrial societies with their immense bureaucracies, operating like huge neural networks in the society at large, in industry, in trade unions, and in practically every other institution, do not provide the individual with the companionship, the sense of participation, and the sense of significance which he requires for his well-being. He is a mere number, a client, a cog, a member of an age-group, a holder of an insurance card. In the cold impersonal world, he needs the warmth of co-operation; in a society so large that he cannot grasp it adequately, except in times of crisis, he wants to be implicated in an enterprise which has caught his imagination. To use a repellent phrase which we owe to Professor Sherif: his ego is not involved; he longs for ego-involvement.

The moralists, too, are vocal. They are saying much the same kind of thing that Durkheim[2] said fifty years ago. In a small compact society, the pressure of public opinion constrains the individual member to keep to the rules. He feels his membership, he identifies himself with the group and the group-ideals become part of him. The bonds of membership in the large-scale society are loose, he does not feel them in the same way, he is faced by what Durkheim called 'anomie' – the absence of an orderly ethos. The constraints are external, not internal; they are embodied in the police force, not in the looks of approval or disapproval of companions, whose goodwill is a worth-while reward. No wonder, it is said, he falls back on his own self-interest as it appears to him at the moment. And moreover, it is suggested, he is not quite happy in so doing.

All this may be somewhat exaggerated, but one cannot ignore such widespread views. In so far as they do depict the plight of the lonely member of our great societies, they make it understandable that a correction should be sought in the exploration of human interaction, in the emphasis of human social needs, and in the concentration of attention on to the social defects of the world in which we live. For this reason *social* psychology has become a focus of interest. Without its being explicitly realized, social psychology is, one might say, in the air, influencing the outlook of people who have never heard of the subject as a scientific discipline. For this reason also the pronouncements of the social psychologist may often seem to be elaborate ways of saying what is in the minds of everyone.

The 'application' of the principles worked out by the psychologists who have paid special attention to group dynamics is, therefore, as so often happens in psychology, a matter of codifying and making explicit ideas and attitudes which are already current, and the very activity of codifying and emphasizing these ideas automatically makes them the more current as the interchange between the social psychologist and the general public proceeds.

If the close relationship between what the social scientist is interested in and what everyone else is interested in be accepted, an important corollary follows. We have renounced the hope that social psychology will tell us something entirely new. We must now admit that some of the principles enunciated may be true of a society in a particular stage of its development, but not universally true of mankind. We have already insisted that groups are part of, and embedded in, a wider culture, and what may be true of groups in one culture may not be true of groups in another. For this reason we ought not to accept without reservation all the views expressed by American social psychologists as being applicable to groups in Great Britain. This in no way means that we can afford to ignore their views. On the contrary, assuming they hold for American society, that itself is of interest, and in any case they give us a lead for social psychological research in Great Britain. The only point is that we may be faced with a double task: the analysis of group activity in different cultures, and a further analysis of cross-cultural differences.

To return now to the research itself and its application. We learn from it, or perhaps, in view of what has been said, we ought to say: we are reminded by it, that people are greatly influenced in their behaviour by the presence of other people as co-members of a group, as co-operators, as competitors, or simply as witnesses. One of the ways in which they are influenced is that they are, as it were, pulled into the value system of the group, made less extreme in their judgements, and anxious to avoid deviating so far from the group standards that they run the risk of ostracism. If they work together on an enterprise they grow to like one another, provided they are on an equal footing; in so far as they feel they are being 'bossed about' they tend to dislike the 'boss'. They seem to enjoy co-operation more than competition, and are prepared to put forth greater efforts if they are members of a team than they would if they were working on their own. They enjoy the companionship of like-minded fellows, and find such companionship a stabilizing influence; it provides them with a collectively accepted frame of reference for their judgements and their perception of the world outside them.

On theoretical grounds, backed up by general observation and by clinical study, we may think of an individual as primarily a social product. He needs interaction for the development of his personality, and in a sense we may say that the wider the range of interaction, the richer the personality will become. This, however, must be corrected by the reflection that some kinds of interaction, so far from enlarging and enriching the personality, stunt it and distort it. More correctly one should say that over-protection in childhood and under-protection in the same period produce personalities who find interaction with other people difficult in later years. They tend to be over-demanding, or suspicious, or hostile, or domineering. They tend, that is to say, to be pre-occupied with their own problems, with the meaning of a situation for *them*, rather than with the people with whom they are interacting. The result is that they bring a distorted view of other people with them, and so far from a wider range of potentialities being actualized, their suspiciousness, demandingness, overbearing, and hostility tend to get further embedded within them. It is not therefore interaction as such that provides the occasion for expansion; it is interaction in which each party respects the other.

In addition we must not allow any stress upon the creative function of interaction to make us under-estimate the creative powers of the individual himself. When self-consciousness has developed he is enabled to reflect on his behaviour, to recombine his experience, to question the standards put before him and to modify them. It may be, as will be suggested below, that this creativeness demands special conditions for its development.

The principles of group dynamics have been applied, in the sense in which we have used this term, to a large number of different fields of human activity: to education, to the technique of psychotherapy, to industry, and to the general running of societies. There are specialist studies of two of these fields already included in this series, and it will not be necessary to deal with them in turn. A rather different, and more general, approach will be made.

Broadly speaking the aims of those who are concerned with the application of group theory to everyday life are of three kinds: the easing of human relations; the enrichment of human personality; and getting people to do things they would not otherwise do. These aims frequently overlap, but it is convenient to deal with them separately.

The easing of human relations may take two forms: discovering what makes them go wrong, and finding out how to make them go right. It is now a commonplace that personal relations often go wrong because of the personal resentments and hostilities which individuals bring with them into any given situation. This links adult difficulties up with the experiences of childhood. But apart from deep-seated personal traits which embitter social intercourse, there are innumerable hazards which affect people who are not more than usually awkward. There are the almost inevitable irritations of everyday life which make us cross, and tempt us to discharge our spleen on some innocent target. If we are not careful, hostility becomes cumulative, and, as industrial psychologists have often pointed out, we almost cease to be aware of its origin. We get angry about something, we cannot express our anger directly, we blame the canteen, and when all we have asked for is granted – we are still enraged. Social good manners, admirable in their way as emollients, often prevent our owning even to ourselves, let alone to anyone else, the cause of our frustration. We resent someone else getting a higher salary, but we can't say so; we feel slighted because a decision has been made over our heads, but of course we are too sensible *really* to mind about a little thing like that. The management of a factory may with the best will in the world decide that joint consultation must be made a reality in the works. They have read all the books; they are convinced. 'With reasonable human beings like ourselves. . . .' And yet discussions get side-tracked, tempers get frayed, and everybody else seems to behave very childishly. The situation is common enough, but the causes are by no means clear until one has read Jaques' *Changing Cultures of a Factory*.[3]

It is now quite clear that a good deal of human interaction is bedevilled by unconscious attitudes and that they will not improve until these are brought out into the open.

Coming nearer the surface, there are often simple defects in the chain of communication of which something has been said already.

Finally human relations are soured by the simple fact that nowadays people do not like being ordered about and resent being, as they think, exploited. This is one of those generalizations which almost certainly is applicable to our own culture but not necessarily applicable elsewhere. In a caste society or semi-caste society the underlings may accept their inferior position and expect to be ordered about. Today the doctrine of equality has taken root, and it is no longer true. People want to participate, not merely to obey arbitrary orders.

This has led to all those schemes of profit-sharing, joint consultation, explanations to the workers, and so forth. It is responsible, too, for the elaborate technique of training for foremanship, often employing the socio-drama technique in which foremen take the part of workers and act out a scene, whereby they become more aware of what it feels like to be 'told off'. The union officials of the Rubber Workers' C.I.O. are said to use the socio-drama in order to get a clearer understanding of the problem of management. Such devices undoubtedly do something to reduce animosity, and ease the situation, but those who pin their faith on solving industrial problems by making factories more cosy must remember that the workers are not immune from the general clashes between the interests of labour and those of capitalism which go on in the outside world.

Most effort is expended in finding out why human relations go wrong, but Stuart Chase, in his *Roads to Agreement*,[4] wisely insists that we should attend to situations in which they go right. He includes among these the joint consultations and other measures which have been mentioned above. He also bids us take heed of the methods used by the Quakers: the composure of silent reflection, the doctrine of unanimity, which will be reached when the 'right' decision presents itself, and the technique of putting controversial matters to one side when it is obvious that no agreement can be reached at any particular moment.

He reminds us, too, that deep-seated differences can often be resolved if the opponents can be induced – or are forced – to co-operate in some activity which is not related to their disagreements. In *The American Soldier*,[5] that compendium of information about the American Army in World War II, we are told that whereas white soldiers who had no experience of fighting alongside Negroes voted 90 per cent against their being in the same brigade, those who had fought in the same company with them voted 86 per cent in favour of continuing the arrangement. Chase tells the story of villages in Lebanon, torn by feuds, achieving peace when an American social scientist got the inhabitants to play volley ball with mixed teams.

Methods of discussion are studied and practised at summer meetings held in the New England town of Bethel, where all kinds of people from offices, factories, social service agencies, the army, the navy, the air force and so on come together to practise conference techniques in training groups and 'active' groups, while 'trained observers sit poker-faced in the background taking notes'. The notes are then processed by the research department upstairs. Stuart Chase, who gives a lively description of this procedure, in which theory and practice go side by side, is a student of semantics among other things. One may hope that he will appreciate the fact that to readers in Great Britain the word 'Bethel' carries with it somewhat dubious overtones.

This consideration of human relations, their difficulties, and what can be done to make them smoother, is the scientific spearhead of the general movement towards the adjustment of disagreements. It is inspired not only by a desire to ease human relations at what one might call the ground-floor level, but also by wider considerations. It is held by some people that war is, in part at any rate, due to the need men have of ridding themselves of the accumulated hostility caused by the frustrations of everyday life. If, therefore, the argument runs, there is less hostility because human interaction runs more smoothly in the home and elsewhere, then the chances of war are diminished. It was this doctrine that lay at the back of the so-called 'Tensions-Project' of UNESCO, in which social scientists were invited to study tensions in various parts of the world, and to advise on their diminution.

It is not easy to assess the cogency of the argument. If people are angry their anger may be deflected on to a scapegoat. If people are unhappy they can be induced to fight by promise of relief when the putative cause of their misery is defeated. No doubt this is so, but there is a danger of confusing what goes on at the ground-floor level with the considerations which weigh with high-level administration. We may assume that the same forces play their part at Cabinet meetings, at conferences of Foreign Ministers, and at meetings of the Presidium in the Kremlin, as are operative at meetings of the Rural District Council or at sessions of a University Senate. The two types of situation are, however, different in one vital respect. At the high level the persons who are sitting round the table have the duty to defend their country from attack, to ensure its prosperity, and to preserve or enhance its position in the world.

Furthermore, they operate within a field of discourse in which war is always a possible method of attaining their ends or of forestalling disasters. It is this that makes the difference. The local

R.D.C. is a representative body, so is the University Senate, but the responsibilities of such bodies are negligible compared with the responsibilities and powers of governments. One cannot help feeling that even if every child were free from aggression, if every village got its houses and its drainage, and if every department got all its claims satisfied – and no one can deny that this would be desirable – nevertheless it would not make much difference to government decisions about war. To believe that a reduction of tension in everyday life will automatically lead to a reduction of tensions between nations is to be sadly unrealistic.

The second aim in the minds of people who seek to apply the results of social psychological investigation was described as 'the enrichment of the personality'. This expression is intended to include not only the development of many sides of the personality by social intercourse on a more extended scale, but also the reduction of insecurity by providing a more companionable social environment. This is where the distinction between the 'external system' and the 'internal system', between the 'socio-group' and the 'psyche-group' come in. The idea is simple: people like companionship, they want to be supported, their difficulties often spring from some form of insecurity, and this can be reduced by friendship. If this is the case, we ought to take more trouble about it. We ought to put people who like one another together, we ought to devise ways of bringing people together, we must even consider sacrificing efficiency to ensuring that people are happy together. This note of providing opportunities for companionship sounds through the contributions which compose a recent book on *Social Group Work*.[6] The climate has changed. In the past the youth clubs aimed at getting boys and girls off the streets and persuading them to engage in activities that the middle classes thought reputable. The extra-curricular educational services aimed at education. Any group was supposed to *do* something worth while. The experts in social group work now take the line that it is nothing to be ashamed of, if the members of these groups just enjoy a good gossip. In an age in which work, worth-while work, is exalted as one of the supreme values of life, it is hard for us to pay much attention to the mere enjoyment of companionship. May it not involve one of the greatest sins in the capitalist calendar: *waste of time*. Pre-literate people would seem to have different, and, perhaps, less dubious values.

This is not, of course, to deprecate activities, and merely to reverse the values of work and enjoyment of company. While groups of friends may meet for the sheer enjoyment of conversation, most organized groups come together for a more definite purpose, and it is the pursuit of such purposes that helps to hold them together. This has certain practical implications. The neighbourhood groups of Chinese cities undoubtedly derive much of their vigour from the clearly obvious tasks to be accomplished: keeping down the flies, keeping the alleys clean, reducing illiteracy, and so on. So it is with many groups in industry all over the world. So it is in such neighbourhood groups as emerge in Britain under threat of aerial bombardment or in times of national festivity. The collective effort and the breaking down of barriers which occur on such occasions has led many people to think that such street or neighbourhood groups might do much to control delinquency. This is, as has been mentioned, the aim of the Chicago Area Project Scheme. The difficulty, however, is that there is nothing obvious to do, as there is in times of crisis or when the street is to be decorated in honour of a Coronation. Perhaps if the neighbours felt deeply about delinquency, something might be done, but to form groups for a purpose, the purpose itself must be clear and the means of attaining it pretty obvious. An active purpose, then, may be essential for the formation of groups; the point is that the provision of opportunity for purely social intercourse should not be thought of as something second-rate.

This is the place to give a bare mention of group psychotherapy. It is not so much a matter here of providing opportunities for expansion, as reducing unsatisfactory contractions. In the group the patient realizes that he or she is not alone, their reaction in conversation gives clues to the therapist, and the group situation itself prepares them for more stable relations with other people.

Group therapy usually means the treatment of a comparatively small number of people at the same time. The therapeutic value of participation in a hospital as a whole has also been found efficacious, while a remarkable book on *The Mental Hospital*[7] describes an institution in America in which the interaction of everyone with everyone else, patients and staff alike, is considered from a therapeutic point of view. Here we have, without the terminology being used, an 'external system': the organization, staffing, financing, and treatment of patients, giving rise to a complex 'internal system' in which the patients are not thought of as objects of therapy alone, but also as participating in an interactive network.

So far we are reminded that there are difficulties in human relations which can now be more satisfactorily traced and more skilfully removed, and that in a society in which so much of the social intercourse is impersonal, some provision should be made to replace the smaller units of which society used to be formed but which – with the exception of the small-scale nuclear family – now cease to provide the sense of security they are alleged to have provided in the past.

The third aim mentioned was: getting people to do things they otherwise would not do. It is here that we venture into rather dangerous waters. Members of groups tend to be drawn into conformity. If a group can be induced to set a target of production, of behaviour, or even of allegiance to a doctrine, then the individual member will be constrained to conform. Such are the levers of manipulation.

Although the evidence is not easy to come by, it is worth considering the application of these principles in the People's Republic of China and in the U.S.S.R. The present writer has had the opportunity of visiting both countries, and of discussing the problem with people who have actually participated in what has already been called 'collective committal' and in meetings of 'Criticism and Self-Criticism'. In the Municipal Prison at Peking they house about ten prisoners in each tiny cell who work in the factories of which the prison is, in a sense, composed, making soap, printing and binding books, making textiles and socks, and doing repairs to the fabric. In one set of cells the inmates were sitting on the broad shelf that served as a bed, discussing. In the soap factory groups of ten and fourteen were sitting in circles inside and out in the yard. In the early hours of the morning the workers at the railway station could be seen sitting in circles, discussing. At the Temple of Heaven, soldiers were sitting in circles on the broad processional way, not playing cards, but discussing.

On inquiry it appeared that practically everyone belongs to some organization or other, and often to more than one. There are occupational groups, intellectual groups, women's groups, and the neighbourhood groups described in Chapter 6. Then there are quasi-political groups such as the Party and Youth organizations like the Young Pioneers. Thus a man in a factory or an office belongs to the shop or department in which he works, to the factory or office to which his shop or department belongs, to his neighbourhood groups, and, possibly, to the Party. Meetings are held at all levels, and of all types of group. The emphasis may lie on production, efficiency, and organization, or on a mutual examination of conduct. From some of the literature which has been translated one gets the impression that men and women hardly stop attending meetings. Where the emphasis lies on production and efficiency the participants commit themselves to greater efforts; where emphasis lies on the examination of conduct, backsliding is checked. The latter type of meeting has a somewhat therapeutic character. The Chinese intellectuals who spoke English were anxious that no false impression should be conveyed. '"Criticism",' they said, 'sounds hostile. Where hostility creeps in, the whole purpose of criticism and self-criticism is lost. We try to explain to people that their mistakes are due to their having been brought up under Feudalism, and we try to make them understand that all this has changed in the New China.' The power of such intensified public opinion was illustrated when a young teacher, who had studied philosophy at Glasgow, admitted that he could not accept Dialectical Materialism in its totality. He was obviously upset by this. 'My fellow workers,' he said, 'are more progressive than I am, but if I persevere I may catch up.' There was no fear expressed; had he been afraid he could easily under the circumstances have 'put on an act'. He was simply wretched because he felt outside the group.

Intellectuals would admit that at first such meetings were painful. Professors had to listen to criticism from their students and colleagues. After a while, they said, they got used to it and found it positively invigorating. A case was reported of a meeting in an office. The manager took the chair and said with all humility that he could find nothing to blame in his recent conduct, whereupon an office boy rose up and told him that he had behaved bureaucratically, telling them nothing about what was happening and so on. The manager got a little hot, and admitted his offences. We are reminded of reports of meetings of the Oxford Group, where the same technique appears to have been used to ensure salvation as is used in China to promote social service.

It is not easy to determine how widespread, and, more particularly, how efficacious these meetings are. The traveller meets enthusiasts, and has to guess. One would expect them to be more efficacious among the proletariat and the intellectuals than among the 'petite bourgeoisie', who keep small shops and small industrial plants, or among the 'national bourgeoisie', the remnants of big capitalist enterprises. In the country districts one would expect them to be more seriously taken by the activists in the villages than by the bulk of the population. Above all, as in the Soviet Union, one would expect such meetings to be more significant for members of the Party and affiliated organizations than for anyone else. In China as in the Soviet Union, the Party and such Youth organizations as the Young Pioneers set out to give an example of devotion to social duty. In both countries they are alive to the insidious dangers of power; in both countries they are sensitive to the opportunities of self-seeking and domineering which bureaucracy provides. You cannot go to a music hall in the Soviet Union without seeing the bureaucrat pilloried.

Even if the bulk of the population living in villages are untouched by these methods of social constraint to conform, one gets the impression that the active and influential members of society are deeply affected by them. A tremendous force of collective conscientiousness is engendered.

In both countries people are being induced to participate. When it comes to participation it is worth while considering the grounds on which the Soviet Union claims to be essentially democratic. Where there is no opposition of interests there can be no parties. At the same time, each unit in the country has its own problems and special needs. You must therefore have representatives from every constituency to put its case to the Soviet immediately above. The area covered by this will be represented in the next Soviet in the hierarchy. The constituents must pick upon the best spokesman, and having found him, an election will usually give him the required 51 per cent of the votes, though it sometimes happens that the person recommended by those who choose the candidate is not elected. In such a case there must be another election. In any case, it is argued, the candidate is chosen after much deliberation, his function is to do the best for his constituency, and if he is found wanting he can be recalled.

Such a system reminds one of our own local government procedure in rural areas, where 'politics' are on the whole in abeyance. The Soviet authorities argue that the deliberations which precede the choice of a candidate, the fact that he is there to put forward the special needs of his district, and the discussions which take place to determine what these needs are, is what the Americans might call 'democracy at the grass roots', and in a sense more participant than the election of a member of a national party.

For the outsider it is difficult to determine how far in such elections people really feel they are participating. It is also difficult to know how far the elections are rigged by the central authority. In spite of one's ignorance of this, the theory and the system which is based upon it is not without interest. Whatever may be true about the Soviet Union, it is not inconceivable that you may have a country in which there is no nation-wide opposition of interests, and only minor disagreements about policy. In such a case the 'party system' becomes a matter simply of the 'ins' and the 'outs'; interest in elections is almost bound to flag. One way of meeting this would be to induce people to take a livelier interest in local affairs. This, of course, does not touch public policy at high levels. Would it not be possible, asks Erich Fromm, to have these discussed at the local level and have a lower house consisting of delegates who would bring with them the views of the groups they represent?

The point of this digression is merely to raise the issue of participation in government. If it be true that when people feel they are participating they are more prepared to put themselves out than is the case when they feel they are simply being ordered about by 'them', then if there are no oppositional issues to arouse interest, something else must be found.

One of the 'something elses' is, of course, the arousal by propaganda and by the devices we have been discussing to produce strong unified public opinion. To put the best face on it we may say that in so far as it works it gives people some sense of participating in a great enterprise, it may provide a certain sense of security by the virtual abolition of choice, it is certainly likely to improve output and efficiency. Our prejudices against Communist countries ought not to blind us to these advantages. We may say that these powerful social psychological weapons are used to bad purpose, but if the critics who say this were to hear of similar methods to induce a heightened patriotism or a return to religious faith, would they demur?

We are confronted with a difficult problem. To repeat what has been said already: such evidence as we have seems to point to the fact that a great many people would relish a closer association with other people in purposive groups in which they have a sense of significance. In these they would cease to be lonely and unimportant, and the very conformity with the group would provide them with standards of conduct from which they and the community might benefit.

Is the study of group-dynamics not only an interesting occupation; not only a symptom of the condition of society, does it also promise a cure for our ills?

Erich Fromm, in his book, *The Sane Society*,[8] does not, by any means, attack the developments of group psychology. He does, however, attack contemporary society in relevant terms. In his view, and it re-echoes and carries forward the view expressed in his *Fear of Freedom*,[9] we have made production an end in itself instead of a means to happiness, we have become parts of machines instead of masters of them, we are commodities for sale, we are what he calls 'alienated' from our 'true' selves. In our subjection to the colossus we have produced we only feel secure in being as similar as possible to our fellow men. 'Any deviation from the pattern, any criticism, arouse fear and insecurity; one is always dependent on the approval of others, just as a drug addict is dependent on his drug, and similarly one's own sense of self and self-reliance becomes ever increasingly weaker.'

We get a picture of what life might be like on a housing estate if the planners who want us all to 'muck in' together had their way, from a description quoted by Fromm of a settlement outside Chicago, called 'Park Forest'. It seems to provide its inhabitants with such a sense of support that other environments seem unduly cold. The standards are bound up with indiscriminate sociability, which is known as 'being *outgoing*'. It brings its own anxieties. A mother is quoted as saying: "Johnny has not been doing so well at school. The teacher told me he was doing fine in some respects but that his social adjustment was not as good as it might be. He would pick one or two friends to play with – and sometimes he was happy to remain by himself."'

This deviant desire to be alone leads to all sorts of little tricks. In order to get a little privacy, we are told, some people move their chairs to the front rather than the court side of the apartment. But when they do this they feel guilty, and are thought of as indulging in some childish prank, or even as suffering from some mild inner neurosis. They are, in fact, 'imprisoned in brotherhood'. The charge of neurosis under such circumstances is, in Fromm's view, misplaced.

'Mental health,' he says, 'is characterized by the ability to love and to create, by the emergence from incestuous ties to clan and soil, by a sense of identity based on one's experience of self as the subject and agent of one's powers.' (p. 69.)

In his discussion of the 'sane society' which is to cure 'alienation' and ensure mental health, Fromm speaks with approval of many findings and developments which we might call the 'application' of modern group psychology: the advantages of small groups in industry, the furthering of human solidarity, the work communities in France, Belgium, Switzerland, and Holland. In his *Fear of Freedom* he wrote: 'Unless the person feels that he belongs somewhere, unless his life has some meaning and direction, he would feel like a particle of dust and be overcome by his insignificance.'

198

There is no question of denouncing the main themes of group dynamics here. And yet it may well be that the application of some of the principles – the powers generated by group committal and the delights of conformity – might well serve to lessen 'one's experience of self as the subject and agent of one's powers'.

Dr Fromm would appear to believe that there is some central core of self, present from the start, which is bound to rebel against pressure to conform. This is an assumption which we have rejected. We have to envisage an application of certain principles of group psychology which would tie people up in cosy little groups, active, participating and conforming – and happy in so doing. This 'danger', if it be a 'danger' is envisaged by Kurt W. Bach,[10] himself a distinguished social psychologist, in an article bearing the significant title: 'Group Addiction'. He mentions the lure of the group, the dislike of the deviant, the inability of members of a group 'to evaluate fellow-members on their merits', they evaluate them rather 'by how well these members relate to the group and what their position is on relevant issues'.

Would it be disastrous if we so perfected our knowledge and our methods that we could produce conforming group-addicts? Dr Fromm dismisses the criterion of happiness, using the dangerous argument that people may think they are happy when 'really' they are not. The only arguments against such a society are that it might well diminish the supply of artistic and scientific geniuses upon which civilization in the past has depended, and that it would inevitably set limits to the variety of potentialities which individuals could develop.

If we seek, as surely it is reasonable to do, to provide for the expansion of all the richness of variety which human beings are capable of displaying we must see to it that our application of such principles of group dynamics as we may discover should safeguard individual differences. By paying serious attention to such principles we may indeed be able to ease human relations, but it would be unfortunate if they were used in such a way as to provide a substitute for what Fromm calls our 'incestuous ties to clan and soil'.

In the modern literature of group psychology one detects, perhaps unfairly, a stressing of the charms of group membership, without much attention being paid to the development of the members themselves. There are, after all, in our society innumerable groups of friends who enjoy companionship and participation in discussion and in co-operative activity, and whose standards include the welcoming and the encouragement of one another's differences. Let us hope that in future research this note will be struck. Enforced groupings in the past have no doubt been restrictive of human development. If we misapply our skills we may produce groups equally restrictive, but in a painless way. On the other hand there is no earthly reason why this should be so if we take as our guide groups of friends rather than groups collectively committed to increased production.

REFERENCES

A great deal of the experimental material dealing with small groups has been collected into three volumes:

1. *Readings in Social Psychology*, edited by T. M. Newcomb and E. L. Hartley (New York, Holt, 1947; second revised edition, 1952). This second edition is referred to below as *Readings*.
2. *Group Dynamics*, ed. D. Cartwright and A. F. Zander (London, Tavistock Publications, 1955). This is referred to as *C and Z*.
3. *Experimental Social Psychology*, by G. Murphy, L. B. Murphy, and T. M. Newcomb (New York, Harper, 1937). This is referred to as *M. M. and N.*

The titles of periodicals are abbreviated as follows:

Amer J Psychol	American Journal of Psychology (Austin, Texas)
Amer J Sociol	American Journal of Sociology (Chicago)
Amer Psychol	American Psychologist (Washington, D.C.)
Amer Sociol Rev	American Sociological Review (New York)
Appl Anthrop	Applied Anthropology (Cambridge, Mass.)
Brit J Delinq	British Journal of Delinquency (London)
Brit J Psychol	British Journal of Psychology (London)
Brit J Sociol	British Journal of Sociology (London)
Hum Org	Human Organization (New York)
Hum Rel	Human Relations (London)
J Abn Soc Psychol	Journal of Abnormal and Social Psychology (Washington, D.C.)
J Accoust Soc Amer	Journal of the Acoustical Society of America (New York)
J Appl Psychol	Journal of Applied Psychology (Washington, D.C.)
J Exp Psychol	Journal of Experimental Psychology (Washington, D.C.)
J Personality	Journal of Personality (Durham, N.C.)
J Soc Issues	Journal of Social Issues (New York)
J Soc Psychol	Journal of Social Psychology (Provincetown, Mass.)
Psychol Rev	Psychological Review (Washington, D.C.)

REFERENCES

Pub Op Quart   Public Opinion Quarterly (Princeton, N.J.)
Soc Rev   Sociological Review (Ledbury, Herefordshire)
Z f Angew Psych   Zeitschrift für Experimentelle und Angewandte
    Psychologie (Göttingen)

CHAPTER 1

1. Smith, M. 'Social Situation, Social Behavior, Social Group', *Psychol Rev*, vol. 52 (1945), pp. 224–9 (*C and Z*, p. 40).
2. Deutsch, M. (*C and Z*, p. 330).
3. Scheidlinger, S. (*C and Z*, p. 56).
4. *Social Organization* (New York, Scribner, 1909), p. 23.

CHAPTER 2

1. Piaget, J. *The Child's Conception of Physical Causality* (London, Kegan Paul, 1930), p. 128.
2. *The First Five Years of Life* (London, Methuen, 1940), p. 31.
3. *ib.*, p. 33.
4. *ib.*, p. 37.
5. (Chicago University Press, 1934).
6. *Human Society* (New York, Macmillan, 1948), p. 211.
7. *ib.*, p. 213.
8. Singh, J. A. L., and Zingg, R. M., *Wolf-Children and Feral Man* (New York, Harper, 1939).
9. Riesman, D. *The Lonely Crowd* (New Haven, Yale University Press, 1950).
10. This experiment has been frequently described and analysed. A brief account by Ronald Lippitt and Ralph K. White will be found in *Readings*, p. 340, where a list of references is also given.
11. *Social Development in Young Children* (London, Routledge, 1933).
12. (London, Kegan Paul, 1932).
13. Hartshorn, H., and May, M. A. *Studies in the Nature of Character* (New York, Macmillan, 1929–30), p. 374.
14. Unpublished Ph.D. Thesis for the University of London: 'A Study of Value-judgements in Adolescents', 1955.
15. Lerner, Eugene. *Moral Judgment in Children* (Monasha, Wis., Baxter, 1937).
16. MacRae, D., jnr. 'The Development of Moral Judgment in Children', unpublished Ph.D Thesis for Harvard University, 1950.

REFERENCES

CHAPTER 3

1. Kelley, Harold H. 'Communication in Experimentally Created Hierarchies', *Hum Rel*, vol. 4 (1951), pp. 39–56 (*C and Z*, p. 443).
2. Thibaut, John. 'An Experimental Study of the Cohesion of Under-privileged Groups', *Hum Rel*, vol. 3 (1950), pp. 251–78 (*C and Z*, p. 102).
3. Moreno, J. L. *Who Shall Survive?* (revised edn., Beacon, N.Y., Beacon House, 1953).
4. Sherif, M., *et al. Social Psychology of the Cross Roads* (New York, Harper, 1951).
5. See Lewin, K., *Resolving Social Conflicts* (New York, Harper, 1948) and *Field Theory in Social Science* (London, Tavistock Publications, 1952). There is also an admirable survey of 'Field Theory in Social Psychology' by Morton Deutsch in Lindzey Gardner (ed.), *Handbook of Social Psychology* (Cambridge, Mass., Addison-Wesley, 1954).
6. Wright, H. F., and Barker, R. G. *Methods in Psychological Ecology* (University of Kansas, 1950).
7. Festinger, L., Schachter, S., and Back, K. *Social Pressure in Informal Groups* (New York, Harper, 1950).
8. Deutsch, M. See note 5 above.
9. (London, Routledge & Kegan Paul, 1951).

CHAPTER 4

1. (Penguin Books, Harmondsworth, 1954).
2. *Life in a Welsh Countryside* (Cardiff, University of Wales Press, 1950). Free Press.
3. *Essays in Sociological Theory Pure and Applied* (Glencoe, Ill., Free Press, 1949).
4. *Exploring English Character* (London, Cresset, 1955), p. 44.
5. *The Social Medicine of Old Age* (Nuffield Foundation; Cambridge University Press, 1947).
6. *Growing Up in the City* (Liverpool University Press, 1954), p. 93.
7. Young, Michael, and Willmott, Peter. *Family and Kinship in East London* (London, Kegan Paul, 1957).
8. Gorer, G., and Rickman, J. *The People of Great Russia* (London, Cresset, 1949).
9. Rees, *op. cit.*, pp. 65, 68, 70.

REFERENCES

10. Arensberg, C. M. *The Irish Countryman* (London, Macmillan, 1937).

11. cf. Mead, Margaret. *Coming of Age in Samoa* (Harmondsworth, Penguin Books, 1944).

12. Slater, E., and Woodside, M. *Patterns of Marriage* (London, Cassell, 1951).

13. The difference in husband-wife relationships as a function of their mobility and consequent detachment from local kin and friends is discussed by Elizabeth Bott in *Family and Social Network* (London, Tavistock Publications, 1957).

14. Mays, *op. cit.*, p. 86.

15. *The Dock Worker* (Liverpool University Press, 1954), pp. 48, 49, 54.

16. Gorer, G. *The Americans* (London, Cresset, 1948).

17. Spinley, B. M. *The Deprived and the Privileged* (London, Routledge and Kegan Paul, 1953), pp. 78, 81.

18. Young, M. 'Income within the Family', *Brit J Sociol*, vol. 3 (1952), p. 318. An article summarizing work done on family budgeting.

19. Professor Madge has kindly given me permission to quote from unpublished research.

20. (London, Routledge & Kegan Paul, 1954), vol. I, part 3.

21. *ib.* p. 167.

22. Lees, J. P. 'Social Mobility of a Group of Eldest-born and Inter-mediate Adult Males', *Brit J Psychol*, vol. 43 (1952), p. 210.

23. Lees, J. P., and Newsom, L. J. 'Family or Sibship Position and some Aspects of Juvenile Delinquency', *Brit J Delinq*, vol. 5 (1954).

24. Davis, A., and Havighurst, Robert J. 'Social Class and Color Differences in Child-Rearing', *Readings*, p. 539.

25. *The Social Background of Delinquency*. Unpublished; available on application to the Librarian, University of Nottingham.

26. *op. cit.*, p. 91.

27. *op. cit.*, p. 68.

28. Robb, James H. *Working-Class Anti-Semite* (London, Tavistock Publications, 1954), p. 61.

29. (University of Chicago Press, 1936).

30. (University of Chicago Press, 1943).

31. *Spontaneous Youth Groups*, ed. P. H. K. Kuenstler. (University of London Press, 1955), p. 52.

32. Cohen, M. *The Delinquent Boy* (English ed., London, Routledge & Kegan Paul, 1956).

REFERENCES

33. Williams, W. M. *Gosforth* (Routledge & Kegan Paul, London, 1956).
34. Eisenstadt, S. N. 'Youth, Culture and Social Structure in Israel', *Brit J Sociol*, vol. 2 (1951), p. 103.
35. Eisenstadt, S. N. 'African Age Groups', *Africa* (1954), p. 100.

CHAPTER 5

1. (New York, Crowell, 3rd edn, 1940), p. 13.
2. *op. cit.*, p. 56.
3. Loomis, C. P., and Beegle, J. A., *Rural Social Systems* (New York, Prentice-Hall, 1951).
4. Ensminger, Douglas, 'Rural Neighborhoods and Communities', in Taylor, C. C., *et al.*, *Rural Life in the United States* (New York, Knopf, 1955), p. 73.
5. *op. cit.*, p. 76.
6. (East Lansing, State Book Store, 1945).
7. Rees, A. D. *Life in a Welsh Countryside* (Cardiff, University of Wales Press, 1950), p. 142.
8. (Harmondsworth, Penguin Books, 1952).
9. *The Social Structure of a Scottish Community*. Unpublished Ph.D. thesis for the University of Edinburgh.
10. Village conflicts and methods of dealing with them are the subject of Ronald Frankenberg's *Village on the Border* (London, Cohen and West, 1957).
11. *op. cit.*, p. 83.
12. Mitchell, C. Duncan. 'Social Disintegration in a Rural Community', *Hum Rel*, vol. 3 (1950), p. 279.
13. Mitchell, C. Duncan. *Soc. Rev*, vol. 42 (1950).
14. Bonham-Carter, *op. cit.*, p. 141.
15. Homans, G. *The Human Group* (London, Routledge & Kegan Paul, 1951), ch. 13.
16. Quoted in Ashworth, W., *The Genesis of Modern British Town Planning* (London, Routledge & Kegan Paul, 1954), p. 125.
17. Wurzbacher, G., and Pflaus, G. *Das Dorf im Spannigsfeld Industrieller Entwicklung* (Stuttgart, Enke Verlag, 1954).

CHAPTER 6

1. Stein, C. *Toward New Towns for America* (Liverpool University Press, 1951), p. 195; quoted in Kuper, L., *Living in Towns* (London, Cresset, 1953), p. 168.

REFERENCES

2. *The Culture of Cities* (London, Secker and Warburg, 1950), p. 475; quoted in Kuper, *ut supra*, p. 168.
3. *Exploring English Character* (London, Cresset, 1955), p. 53.
4. Rich, D., 'Spare Time in the Black Country', in *Living in Towns, op. supra cit.*, p. 322.
5. See p. 70.
6. *Growing Up in the City* (Liverpool University Press, 1955), p. 47.
7. Hsiao T'ang Fei. *Peasant Life in China* (London, Kegan Paul, 1943), p. 98.
8. From an unpublished MS. by C. Dore.
9. Quoted from the *Annual Report* of 1950–51.
10. Festinger, L., Schachter, S., and Back, K. *Social Pressure in Informal Groups* (New York, Harper, 1950).
11. Merton, R. K. 'The Social Psychology of Housing', in Dennis Wayne (ed.), *Present Trends in Social Psychology* (University of Pittsburgh Press, 1943).
12. Kuper, L. 'Blueprint for Living Together', in *Living in Towns, op. supra cit.*, p. 93.
13. *ib.*, p. 159.
14. *Neighbourhood and Community* (Liverpool University Press, 1954), p. 74.
15. *ib.*, p. 119.
16. *ib.*, p. 138.
17. *ib.*, p. 44.
18. (London, King and Son, 1939).
19. *op. cit.*, p. 141.
20. *op. cit.*, p. 126.
21. *op. cit.*, p. 124.
22. Mann, Peter C. 'The Concept of Neighborliness', *Amer J Sociol*, vol. 60 (1954), p. 163.
23. The standard work on the nineteenth-century American communities is Nordhoff, C., *The Communistic Societies of the United States* (London, Murray, 1875), from which much of the material here cited is drawn.
24. Quoted in Chapin, F. Stuart, *Experimental Designs in Sociological Research* (New York, Harper, revised ed., 1955), p. 7.
25. cf. Unwin, J. D., *Sex and Society* (Oxford University Press, 1934).
26. *op. cit.*, p. 387.
27. See his *Utopia and Experiment* (New York, Praeger, 1955), and *Co-operative Living*, a journal of the Group Farming Research Institute, of which Infield is editor.

REFERENCES

28. *Co-operative Living* (1951), vol. 3, no. 2, p. 10.
29. 'Aizetoro, a Co-operative Community in Nigeria', *Co-operative Living* (1953), vol. 5, no. 3, p. 14.

CHAPTER 7

1. In preparing these chapters I have been greatly indebted to Dr J. Klein of the University of Birmingham. Her book *The Study of Groups* (London, Routledge & Kegan Paul, 1956) is one of the best introductions to recent work on small groups, and for greater detail readers are referred to it.

2. cf. Allport, F. H., *Social Psychology* (Boston, Houghton Mifflin, 1924), p. 262.

3. Laird, D. A. 'Changes in Motor Control and Individual Variations under the Influence of "Ragging"', *J Exp Psychol*, vol. 6 (1923), pp. 236–47.

4. *op. cit.*, note 2, p. 261.

5. Gates, G. S., 'The Effect of an Audience upon Performance', *J Abn Soc Psychol*, vol. 18 (1924), pp. 334–42.

6. Travis, L. F. 'The Effect of a Small Audience upon Eye-Hand Co-ordination', *J Abn Soc Psychol*, vol. 20 (1925), pp. 142–6.

7. Dashiell, J. F., 'An Experimental Analysis of Some Group Effects', *J Abn Soc Psychol*, vol. 25 (1930), pp. 290–9.

8. *op. cit.*, p. 266.

9. Whittemore, I. C., 'Influence of Competition upon Performance', *J Abn Soc Psychol*, vol. 19 (1924), pp. 236–53.

10. Moede, W. *Experimentelle Massenpsychologie* (Leipzig, 1920).

11. Mukerji, N. P. 'An Investigation of Ability in Work in Groups and in Isolation, *Brit J Psychol*, vol. 30 (1939–40), pp. 352–6.

12. Sengupta, N. W., and Sinha, C. P. N. 'Mental Work in Isolation and in Groups', *Indian Journal of Psychology*, vol. 1 (1926), pp. 106–10.

13. Hilgard, E. R., Sait, E. M., and Magaret, G. A. 'Level of Aspirations as Effected by Relative Standing in an Experimental Social Group', *J Exp Psychol*, vol. 27 (1940), pp. 411–21.

14. Allport, F. H., *op. cit.*, p. 277.

15. Wyatt, S., Frost, L., and Stock, F. G. L. 'Incentives in Repetitition Work', Medical Research Council, Industrial Health Board Report, no. 69 (London, H.M.S.O., 1934).

16. Whitehead, T. N. *Leadership in a Free Society* (London, Oxford University Press, 1936), Chap. III.

REFERENCES

17. Lorenz, E. 'Zur Psychologie der industriellen Gruppensarbeit', *Z f Angew Psych*, vol. 45 (1933), pp. 1–45.

18. *The Study of Groups* (London, Routledge and Kegan Paul, 1956).

19. Sherif, M. *An Outline of Social Psychology* (New York, Harper, 1948), Chap. 7.

20. Knight, H. C. A. 'Comparison of the Reliability of Group and Individual Judgments', Master's Thesis, Columbia University, 1921. *M. M. and N.*, p. 710.

21. Gordon, Kate. 'Group Judgments in the Field of Lifted Weights', *J Exp Psychol*, vol. 7 (1924), pp. 398–400.

22. Jenness, A. 'The Role of Discussion in the Change of Opinion', *J Abn Soc Psychol*, vol. 27 (1932), pp. 279–96.

23. Shaw, M. E. 'A Comparison of Individuals and Small Groups in the Rational Solution of Complex Problems', *Amer J Psychol*, vol. 44 (1932), pp. 491–502.

24. Watson, G. R. 'Do Groups Think more of Efficiency than Individuals?', *J Abn Soc Psychol*, vol. 23 (1928), pp. 328–36.

25. Thorndike, R. L. 'The Effect of Discussion upon the Correctness of Group Decision, when the Factor of Majority Influence is Allowed for', *J Soc Psychol*, vol. 9 (1938), pp. 343–62.

26. Gurnee, H. 'Maze Learning in the Collective Situation', *J of Psychol.*, vol. 3 (1937), pp. 437–43; 'A Comparison of Collective and Individual Judgments of Fact', *J Exp Psychol*, vol. 21, (1937), pp. 106–12.

27. Timmons, W. M. 'Can the Product Superiority of Discussion be Attributed to Averaging or Majority Influence?', *J Soc Psychol*, vol. 15 (1942), pp. 23–32.

28. Thorndike, R. L. 'On What Type of Task will a Group do Well?', *J Abn Soc Psychol*, vol. 33 (1938), pp. 409–13.

29. McCreedy, H. G., and Lambert, W. E. 'The Efficiency of Small Human Groups in the Solution of Problems Requiring Genuine Co-operation', *J Personality*, vol. 20 (1952), pp. 478–49.

30. Husband, R. W. 'Co-operative versus Solitary Problem Solution', *J Soc Psychol*, vol. 11 (1940), pp. 405–9.

31. South, E. B. 'Some Psychological Aspects of Committee Work', *J Appl Psychol*, vol. 11 (1927), pp. 348–68, 437–64.

32. Deutsch, M. 'Task Structure and Group Process', *Amer Psychol*, vol. 6 (1951), pp. 324–5.

33. Bechterev, W., and Lange, M. 'Die Ergebnisse Experiments auf dem Gebiete der kollektiven Reflexologie', *Z f Angew Psych*, vol. 24 (1924), pp. 224–54 (*M. M. and N.*, p. 716).

REFERENCES

34. Gibb, J. R. 'The Effects of Group Size and of Threat Reduction upon Creativity in Problem Solving', *Amer Psychol*, vol. 6 (1951), p. 324.

35. Kelley, Harold H., and Thibaut, John W. 'Experimental Studies in Group Problem Solving and Process', in Lindzey, Gardner, (ed.), *Handbook of Social Psychology* (Cambridge, Mass., Addison–Wesley, 1954), ch. 21, p. 773.

36. Carter, L., *et al.* 'The Relation of Categorizations and Ratings in the Observation of Group Behaviour', *Hum Rel*, vol. 4 (1951), pp. 239–54.

37. Bales, R. F., *et al.* 'Channels of Communication in Small Groups', *Amer Sociol Rev*, vol. 16 (1951), pp. 461–8.

38. Stephan, F. F., and Mishler, E. G. 'The Distribution of Participation in Small Groups', *Amer Sociol Rev*, vol. 17 (1952), pp. 598–608.

39. Maier, N. R. F., and Solem, A. R. 'The Contribution of a Discussion Leader to the Quality of Group Thinking', *Hum Rel*, vol. 5 (1952), pp. 277–88 (*C and Z*, p. 561).

40. Mintz, A. 'Nonadaptive Group Behaviour', *J Abn Soc Psychol*, vol. 46 (1951), pp. 150–9 (*Readings*, p. 190).

41. Deutsch, M. 'A Theory of Co-operation and Competition', and 'An Experimental Study of the Effects of Co-operation and Competition upon Group Process', *Hum Rel*, vol. 2 (1949), pp. 129–52, 199–232 (*C and Z*, p. 319).

42. Fouriezos, N. T., Hull, M. L., and Guetzkow, H. 'Measurement and Self-oriented Needs in Discussion Groups', *J Abn Soc Psychol*, vol. 45 (1950), pp. 682–90.

43. Heinicke, C., and Bales, R. F. 'Development Trends in the Structure of Small Groups', *Sociometry* (Beacon, N.Y., 1953), vol. 16, pp. 7–39.

CHAPTER 8

1. Higham, T. M. 'Is Communication a Sacred Cow?', *Personnel Management* (London, 1953), vol. 35, p. 219.

2. Acton Society Trust. *National Industry*, no. 8 (1951).

3. Brown, J. A. C. *The Social Psychology of Industry* (Harmondsworth, Penguin Books, 1954).

4. Bavelas, Alex. 'A Mathematical Model for Group Structures', *Appl Anthrop*, vol. 7 (1948), pp. 16–30; 'Communication Patterns in Task-Oriented Groups', *J Acoust Soc Amer*, vol. 22 (1950), pp. 725–30 (*C and Z*, p. 493).

5. Leavitt, Harold J. 'Some Effects of Certain Communication Patterns on Group Performance', *J Abn Soc Psychol*, vol. 46 (1951), pp. 38–50 (*Readings*, p. 108).

6. Christie, L. S., Luce, R. D., and Macy, J. *Communications and Learning in Task-oriented Groups* (Cambridge, Mass., Research Laboratory of Electronics, 1952).

7. Cambridge, Mass., Addison-Wesley Press. See also: Bales, R. F., 'Some Uniformities of Behaviour in Small Social Systems' (*Readings*, p. 146).

8. Carr, L. J. 'Experimental Sociology', *Social Forces*, vol. 8 (1929), pp. 63–74.

9. Steinzer, B. 'The Development and Evaluation of a Measure of Social Interaction', *Hum Rel*, vol. 2 (1949), pp. 103–22.

10. See Bales, R. F., and Strodtbeck, F. L. 'Phases in Group Problem Solving', *J Abn Soc Psychol*, vol. 46 (1951), pp. 485–95.

11. *Readings*, p. 158.

12. Bales, R. F. 'The Equilibrium Problem in Small Groups', Chap. 4 of Parsons, T., Bales, R. F., and Shils, E. A., *Working Papers in the Theory of Action* (Glencoe, Ill., Free Press, 1953).

13. Strodtbeck, F. 'Husband-Wife Interaction over Revealed Differences', *Amer Sociol Rev*, vol. 16 (1951), pp. 468–73.

14. Jaques, E. *The Changing Culture of a Factory* (London, Tavistock Publications, 1951).

CHAPTER 9

1. Jennings, H. H. *Leadership and Isolation*, 2nd ed. (New York, Longmans Green, 1950). Cf. 'Leadership and Sociometric Choice', in *Readings*, p. 312.

2. Barnard, Chester I. *The Functions of the Executive* (Cambridge, Mass., Harvard University Press, 1951).

3. Horsfall, A. B., and Arensberg, C. M. 'Teamwork and Productivity in a Shoe Factory', *Hum Org*, vol. 8 (1949), pp. 13–25.

4. Simmel, G. *Soziologie* (Munich, Duncker and Humbolt, 2. Auflage, 1922), pp. 59f.

5. Mills, T. M. 'Power Relations in Three-Person Groups', *Amer Sociol Rev*, vol. 18 (1953), pp. 351–67 (*C and Z*, p. 428).

6. cf., e.g., van Zelst, R. H. 'Validation of a Sociometric Regrouping Procedure', *J Abn Soc Psychol*, vol. 47 (1952), pp. 299–301.

7. French, J. P. R., jnr. 'Organized and Unorganized Groups under Fear and Frustration', *University of Iowa Studies in Child Welfare*, vol. 20 (1944), pp. 229–308.

REFERENCES

8. Lippitt, R., Polansky, N., Redl, F., and Rosen, S. 'Dynamics of Power', *Hum Rel*, vol. 5 (1952), pp. 37–64.

9. Bovard, E. W., jnr. 'Experimental Production of Interpersonal Effect', *J Abn Soc Psychol*, vol. 47 (1952), pp. 521–8.

10. Asch, S. E. 'Effects of Group Pressure upon the Modification and Distortion of Judgments', in Guetzkow, H., ed., *Groups, Leadership, and Men* (Pittsburgh, Rutgers University Press, 1951) *Readings*, p. 2).

11. Merei, F. 'Group Leadership and Institutionalization', *Hum Rel*, vol. 2 (1949), pp. 23–39 (*Readings*, p. 318).

12. Schachter, S. 'Deviation, Rejection, and Communication', *J Abn Soc Psychol*, vol. 46 (1951), pp. 190–207 (*C and Z*, p. 223).

13. Whyte, W. F. *Human Relations in the Restaurant Industry* (New York, McGraw Hill, 1948).

14. Jennings, H. H., *op. cit.*

15. Newcomb, T. M. *Personality and Social Change* (New York, Dryden Press, 1943). Cf. 'Attitude Development as a Function of Reference Groups: the Bennington Study' (*Readings*, p. 420).

16. Horowitz, M. W., Lyons, J., and Perlmutter, H. V. 'Induction of Forces in Discussion Groups', *Hum Rel*, vol. 4 (1951), pp. 57–76.

17. Jacobson, E., Charters, W. W., jnr., and Lieberman, S. 'The Use of the Role Concept in the Study of Complex Organizations', *J Soc Issues*, vol. 7 (1951), pp. 18–27.

18. Hemphill, J. K. *Theory of Leadership* (Unpublished Staff Report, Ohio State University, 1952). Cited by C. A. Gibb in Lindzey, Gardner (ed.), *Handbook of Social Psychology* (Cambridge, Mass., Addison-Wesley, 1954), p. 761.

19. Horsfall, A. B., and Arensberg, C. M. 'Teamwork and Productivity in a Shoe Factory', *Hum Org*, vol. 8 (1949), pp. 13–25.

20. cf. Lewin, K., 'Group Decision and Social Change' (*Readings*, p. 459), and Lewin, K., *Field Theory and Social Psychology* (London, Tavistock Publications, 1952).

21. Maier, N. R. F. *Psychology in Industry* (London, Harrap, 1947).

22. Coch, Lester, and French, John R. P., jnr., 'Overcoming Resistance to Change', *Hum Rel*, vol. 1 (1947–8), pp. 512–32 (*Readings*, p. 474).

23. *Readings*, p. 466.

CHAPTER 10

1. Young, Kimball. *Handbook of Social Psychology* (London, Kegan Paul, 1946), p. 387.

2. Miller, N. E., and Dollard, J. *Social Learning and Imitation* (London, Kegan Paul, 1945).

REFERENCES

3. Freud, S. *Group Psychology and the Analysis of the Ego* (London, Hogarth, 1922), p. 80.

4. Sighele, S. *La Foule criminelle* (Paris, Alcan, 1901).

5. Grosser, D., Polansky, N., and Lippitt, R. 'A Laboratory Study of Behavioural Contagion', *Hum Rel*, vol. 4 (1951), p. 115.

6. 'Mass Phenomena', in Lindzey, Gardner, ed., *Handbook of Social Psychology* (Cambridge, Mass., Addison-Wesley, 1954), vol. 2, p. 846.

7. *ib.*, p. 847.

8. Cantril, H. *The Psychology of Social Movements* (New York, Wiley, 1941), p. 94.

9. Cantril, H. 'The Invasion from Mars', *Readings*, p. 198.

10. Paterson, T. T., and Willett, F. J. 'Unofficial Strikes', *Soc Rev*, vol. 43 (1951), p. 57.

11. Gouldner, Alvin W. *Wildcat Strike* (London, Routledge and Kegan Paul, 1955).

12. Scott, J. F., and Homans, G. C. 'Reflections on Wildcat Strikes', *Amer Sociol Rev*, vol. 12 (1947), pp. 278–86.

13. Young, Kimball, *op. cit.*, p. 400.

14. *ib.*, p. 404.

15. Quoted by R. H. Thouless, *An Introduction to the Psychology of Religion* (Cambridge University Press, 1923), p. 153.

16. *ib.*, p. 155.

17. Bion, W. R., 'Experiences in Groups', *Hum Rel*, vol. 1 (1948), pp. 314–20, 487–96; vol. 2 (1949), pp. 13–22, 295–303; vol. 3 (1950) pp. 3–14, 395–402; vol. 4 (1951), pp. 221–7.

18. Shils, E. A. 'Primary Groups in the American Army', in Merton, R. K., and Lazarsfeld, P. F. (eds.), *Continuation in Social Research* (Glencoe, Ill., Free Press, 1950).

19. Stouffer, S. A., *et al.* (ed.) *The American Soldier* (Princeton University Press, 1949), vol. 2, p. 130.

20. Quoted in Sherif, M., and Cantril, H., *The Psychology of Ego-Involvements* (New York, Wiley, 1947), p. 358.

21. *Men Under Stress* (Philadelphia, Blakiston, 1945).

22. Shils, E. A., and Janowitz, M. 'Cohesion and Disintegration in the Wehrmacht in World War II', *Pub Op Quart*, vol. 12 (1948), pp. 280–315.

23. (London, John Bale and Danielson, 1919).

24. Curle, A. 'Transitional Communities and Social Re-connection', *Hum Rel*, vol. 1 (1947–8), pp. 42–68 and 240–88.

25. Bettelheim, B. 'Individual and Mass Behaviour in Extreme Situations', *Readings*, p. 33.

REFERENCES

26. Quoted by Sutherland, E. H., and Cressey, D. R., *Principles of Criminology* (New York, Lippincott, 1955), p. 502.
27. *ib.*, p. 503.
28. Aichhorn, A. *Wayward Youth* (London, Putnam, 1936).
29. Wills, D. *The Hawkspur Experiment* (London, Allen and Unwin, 1941).

CHAPTER 11

1. Cf. Sprott, W. J. H., *Science and Social Action* (London, Watts, 1954), chs. 1 and 8; Merton, R. K., *Social Theory and Social Structure* (Glencoe, Ill., Free Press, 1951), p. 329.
2. Durkheim, E. *Suicide* (London, Routledge & Kegan Paul, 1952).
3. (London, Tavistock Publications, 1951).
4. (London, Phoenix, 1952).
5. Stouffer, S. A., *et al.* (ed.) (Princeton University Press, 1949).
6. Kuenstler, Peter (ed.), *Social Group Work* (London, Faber, 1955).
7. Stanton, A. H., and Schwartz, M. S. *The Mental Hospital* (London Tavistock Publications, 1955).
8. (London, Routledge & Kegan Paul, 1956).
9. (London, Kegan Paul, 1942).
10. *Adult Leadership* (Chicago, Ill.), October 1954, p. 8.

INDEX

215

*Some Pelican books
on allied subjects are described
on the remaining pages*

PSYCHOLOGY IN PELICANS

Pelican books have achieved an enviable reputation for publishing first-class books on psychology for the general reader. Among the titles available are:

MORE PSYCHOLOGY IN PELICANS

Among the other books on psychology published in Pelicans are:

CHILD CARE AND THE GROWTH OF LOVE - A271
John Bowlby and Margaret Fry

HUMAN GROUPS - A346
W. J. H. Sprott

MEMORY: FACTS AND FALLACIES - A405
Ian M. L. Hunter

PSYCHIATRY TODAY - A262
David Stafford-Clark

THE PSYCHOLOGY OF SEX - A194
Oswald Schwarz

THE PSYCHOLOGY OF STUDY - A582
C. A. Mace

THE PSYCHOLOGY OF THINKING - A453
Robert Thomson

THE SOCIAL PSYCHOLOGY OF INDUSTRY - A296
J. A. C. Brown

THINKING TO SOME PURPOSE - A44
Susan Stebbing

Also available in Penguins:

JOURNEY THROUGH ADOLESCENCE - PH60
Doris Odlum